Power Encounter in
Spiritual Warfare

Power Encounter in Spiritual Warfare

Charles H. Kraft

WIPF & STOCK · Eugene, Oregon

POWER ENCOUNTER IN SPIRITUAL WARFARE

Wipf & Stock
An Imprint of Wipf and Stock Publishers
199 W. 8th Ave., Suite 3
Eugene, OR 97401

www.wipfandstock.com

PAPERBACK ISBN: 978-1-5326-1714-0
HARDCOVER ISBN: 978-1-4982-4161-8
EBOOK ISBN: 978-1-4982-4160-1

Manufactured in the U.S.A.   MAY 11, 2017

I DEDICATE THIS BOOK to my former colleague and mentor, Alan Tippettt, to whom we owe the concept of Power Encounter. When I joined the faculty of the School of World Mission at Fuller Seminary in 1969, he was the senior anthropologist and I, his junior. Thus began a friendship and mutual admiration that lasted until his death and included the years after he had retired in 1977 and returned to his beloved Australia.

We taught the same students, wrote for the same audience and for the same cause, went to the same meetings, and encouraged each other, he for choosing to live and work in a land that continued to be foreign to him after many years, and I as I worked to carve out a name for myself in the relatively new discipline called missiology.

His was a great intellect, but he was an able practitioner as well.

His gifts suited him well both to the classroom and to discovering applications in the field. He was a field missionary for two decades in the Fiji Islands, but adept at the academic exercise of developing missiological theory to help us all to understand the significant relationships within and between cultures.

In dedicating this book to Alan I can only hope that my use of his insights is worthy of having his name attached to it. May those who use this book be blessed in using it.

I am grateful to Moody Press and Joan Tippett (for the Tippett family) for permission to quote from Alan's book *People Movements in Southern Polynesia* and to Wipf and Stock for permission to use material from my book *The Rules of Engagement*. I also thank Brian Palmer for his substantial part in shepherding this book through to publication.

Special thanks go to Judy Taber for her help in the final stages.

Contents

Lists of Illustrations or Tables

Preface

I AM SAD FOR the kind of Christianity we have taken to the world as missionaries. I regret the fact that I spent three years myself introducing the church leaders I worked with in northeast Nigeria to a powerless Christianity.

I feel we did much right. The leaders I worked with accepted a Christianity full of love, a life-transforming faith that looked a lot like New Testament Christianity in many ways. But it had been secularized and lacked the kind of power that we see in the New Testament.

We had learned to work within the culture and not against it. This was good and paid off richly so that the estimates of the percentage of Christ-followers in "our" people group (Kamwe— a tribe of around three-quarters of a million) range in the high nineties. But their Christianity, though strong on love, was weak on power. For power we missionaries had taught them to secularize—to depend on clinics and hospitals for healing, and schools for the knowledge they needed to handle most of the human problems. The churches helped many people, especially those who were Westernizing and relating positively to the cultural changes.

But there was a kind of underground of folk answers to daily problems, largely hidden from the missionaries, but very much alive for both Christ-followers and non-Christians. This underground provided fertile ground for Christian witness not unlike that observed by Tippett in the South Pacific. The Nigerian believers, experiencing the freedom of a culture-positive approach felt free to incorporate godly spiritual power into their version of Christianity. This resulted in a more complete, more attractive and more relevant Christianity in this corner of Nigeria.

This Christianity dealt with the spiritual issues that the churches often neglected, issues that the church as a whole had learned from Western missionaries to ignore. But the Nigerian leaders attempted to fill in the gaps left in a secular Christianity and came to a Christianity more like the New Testament version.

This story occurs frequently enough that we can speak of "power encounter Christianity" and note the greater effectiveness of an approach that includes spiritual power over other approaches to witness, especially among animists.

What follows is a discussion of the nature and applicability of power encounter in relation to spiritual warfare. Power encounter was Jesus' method and Jesus applied it, using his power to fight his and our enemy, to show his love. Our aim is that we should learn from the experience in the South Pacific.

I have dedicated the book to Dr. Alan Tippett, who observed, named and studied the concept of power encounter. Power encounter was what the peoples of the South Pacific turned to when missionary Christianity let them down. The same is happening when at least some of the Christians in our day get their freedom and choose to get more in tune with Jesus' way apart from Westernized Christianity.

CHAPTER 1

The Concept of Power Encounter

THE TERM "POWER ENCOUNTER" was coined by Fuller missiologist, the late Alan Tippett to label an event commonly experienced by the peoples of the South Pacific as they converted to Christianity. Tippett noted that people usually had come to Christ in large groupings ("people movements") soon after a major confrontation that tested the power of their ancestral gods against that of the Christian God resulting in an obvious victory for the latter. These encounters were reminiscent of the scriptural encounters between Moses and Pharaoh (Exod 7–12) and Elijah and the prophets of Ba'al (1 Kgs 18).

South Pacific peoples were (and are) keenly aware of the presence, activity and power of spirits. Their leaders were openly committed to the gods of their islands. They credited these gods with providing protection, food, fertility and all other necessities of life for them. But the people also lived in great fear of the anger and vengeance of their gods. To challenge the ancestral gods was unthinkable for most South Pacific peoples. Nevertheless, in turning to Christ, often after years of weighing the potential consequences of challenging the gods, it was chiefs and priests, those who knew the gods and their power best, who chose to challenge them. In doing so, they wagered that the Christian God had greater power than their gods and cast themselves completely on him for protection from the revenge of the god.

A typical power encounter would involve a priest or chief, speaking on behalf of his people, publicly denouncing their allegiance to their god(s) in the name of Jesus and challenging the god(s) to do something about it. When the god(s) could not respond, the victory belonged to Jesus and large numbers of the people usually converted. As Tippett noted, power-oriented people require power proof, not simply reasoning, if they are to be convinced.

The value and validity of an approach to evangelism that involves power confrontations is widely accepted today in missiological thinking and practice, since it is recognized that most of the peoples of the world are power oriented. Current theorists such as myself, however, have expanded Tippett's original concept to include healing and deliverance from demons. We see Jesus' ministry as including numerous such power encounters. These encounters are usually less spectacular than those Tippett described but, it is argued, they qualify as genuine power encounters since they involve the pitting of the power of the true God to bring freedom against the power of Satan designed to keep people in bondage. Furthermore, such "signs and wonders" frequently result in the conversion of families and even larger groups who accept the healing or deliverance as demonstrating the presence and power of God. There is, however, some difference of opinion over whether such encounters should be planned and strategized or simply taken advantage of when they occur.

It is important to note that conversion through power encounter does not assure that the movement will be stable and enduring. Throughout the Scriptures we see that people can observe God's mightiest demonstrations of power but soon go right back to the gods who were defeated. Thus it was both after Moses defeated Pharaoh and Elijah defeated the prophets of Baal. So it has been in many of the power events in the South Pacific and elsewhere. The crucial dimension, as always in conversion, is what happens after the turning, whether people feed and grow their new relationship or neglect it and let it die.

What Tippett found was that the beginnings of the acceptance of Christ in the Pacific islands usually involved encounters between the gods of the people and Christ. When Jesus won such encounters, then, the South Pacific islanders turned to Christ in culturally appropriate larger or smaller groups that we labeled "People Movements." They did not come one by one. Nor were they reasoned into conversion. Culturally they were both group and power oriented. Underlying these movements of people to Christ were power encounters, for "in a power-oriented society, change of faith had to be power-demonstrated" (Tippett, *People Movements*, 81).

Key Point

What we are dealing with is an encounter or confrontation between the false gods and the true God. The power of the true God is demonstrated, the people see that their gods can do nothing against the true God, and the group converts.

This encounter takes place at two levels: the human level and the spirit level. At the spirit level the most powerful God wins and protects the one, the family or the larger group who have defected from the revenge of the weaker god/spirit. At the human level, then, there is defection where a representative of the false god defects either as representing a group or as an individual, desecrating the symbol (e.g., animal, fish, wooden carving) that represents the god, thereby challenging the false god to retaliate in the name and power of Jesus Christ. If there is no retaliation, the true God has won.

A Wider Use of the Concept

Tippett's concern was a historical one. His interest was primarily in the place this concept had in the introduction of Christianity in the South Pacific. Those of us concerned with spiritual warfare in the present, however, have found the concept worthy of wider application. So we have begun using the term with a much broader meaning than Tippett originally envisioned. He saw no problem, though, in our using the concept in this broader way.

We who use the term today use it to label healings, deliverances, or any other visible, practical demonstration that Jesus Christ is more powerful than the spirits, powers, or false gods worshiped or feared by the members of a given people group. The concept of "taking territory" from the enemy for God's kingdom is seen as basic to such encounters and a major method of winning power-oriented people to Christ.

The power encounters in Scripture are between the true God and the gods the Israelites encountered as they took over the promised land. The people of Canaan were classic animists following a plethora of deities attached to trees, bodies of water, land and various other items and places. Usually, though, there was a single deity (often known as Baal) governing the lesser ones. It was that deity who was to be challenged in a power encounter.

There are specific encounters in Scripture in both Old and New Testaments. In the Old Testament we have God against Pharaoh in the deliverance of Israel from Egypt, David against Goliath, Elijah against the prophets of Baal and the success of the Israelite armies when, in faithfulness to God, they went into battle against his spirit enemies. When Israel was unfaithful they usually lost, except when God was avenging himself against the army of Aram in the events recorded in 1 Kgs 20:13–30. In this event, the army of Aram had insulted God by claiming he was a god of the mountains only. So even though the Israelite king was the wicked Ahab, God avenged himself by allowing Israel a victory.

In the New Testament, then, we see Jesus engaging in power encounters by delivering people from evil spirits (Mark 5:1ff.; 9:14ff.; Luke 4:33; 9:37; Matt 8:16; 17:14; etc.), and Jesus' followers doing the same in Acts 4:7–10; 5:16; 8:7; 16:18; etc. In one particularly impressive power encounter, the result was that the converts burned their magical books (Acts 19:19)—books with an incredible monetary value.

Even temptation can be considered a power encounter. Throughout the Old Testament we see Israel facing the constant strong temptation to turn to the animistic gods away from the true God. Prominent examples include Gideon who, after he had won a great victory for Yahweh, retired and returned to the pagan gods of his father. Or Solomon who allowed pagan wives to lead him to follow their gods.

The history of the kings of Israel and Judah, then, is an account of which god or gods the Israelites would follow. And each of the kings has a "report card," evaluating his reign. This report card had but a single entry on it. That entry states whether the king followed Yahweh and was, therefore, a "good" king or whether that king followed the animistic god, and was, therefore, an "evil" king who "sinned against the Lord" (see, e.g., 1 Kgs 16:25–26, 31–33; 2 Kgs 8:18, 27; 10:29–31; etc.). And notice that all of the northern kingdom kings followed animistic gods and several of the kings of the southern kingdom (Judah) fell into the "evil" category as well. And were so labeled according to this single criterion. I conclude that the animism / true God distinction is important to God.

These contests between the true God and counterfeit gods involve encounters in which the superior power of the true God is demonstrated. Thus, Jesus' entire ministry is seen as a massive series of power confrontations between God and the enemy. The continuing ministry of the apostles and their disciples is then seen as the continuance of the exercise of the "authority and power over all demons and all diseases" given by Jesus to his followers (Luke 9:1). And the further taking up of God's power today, encountering demons and defeating them is the fulfillment of Jesus' prediction in John 14:12 that we would do his works and more. We, too, are to proclaim Jesus in power encounters.

We are expected today to use Jesus' approach to witness by participating in these events that we are calling power encounters. The use of power encounters was a prominent means of attracting people to God in Jesus' day. And we have been given the ability to work in Jesus' name as Jesus did—in love and power.

A Passage from Tippett

To illustrate further this important aspect of power witness, we turn to one of Tippett's reports concerning Samoa:

In common with other people of Oceania, the Samoans believed that the only real and effective way of proving the power of their new faith was to demonstrate that the old religion had lost its powers and fears. . . .

The aitu [god] of [King] Malietoa was a fish called anae, a kind of mullet. On the appointed day the forbidden food was set before Malietoa. The incident created tremendous excitement. Friends and distant relatives had come from afar to witness the daring spectacle. Many expected all who ate to drop dead there and then. Those of the family who were to share the experiment were in some cases so frightened that they dowsed themselves with oil and salt water as possible antidotes to the mana [power] of the aitu. But Malietoa and a few others with him took no precautions. As a power encounter it had to succeed or fail on its own merits. By partaking as a social unit the encounter involved both Malietoa as an individual and his family as a group. They ate. The excitement subsided. No evil befell them. Thereafter for many the lotu [Christian faith] was true and the aitu was false. Malietoa's sons could endure the separation for no more than three weeks, and then pleaded for the family's permission to take the same step.

This incident led many people to dispense with their personal aitu or break the taboos, and to put themselves under the instruction of the Christian teachers. The movement gained momentum. Chiefs took the initiative; and thus it was that when [the missionary] Williams arrived after twenty moons, he found villages all around the coast where large groups had eaten or desecrated their aitu, built chapels, and were awaiting the return of Williams with more teachers. Their gods had been discarded, evil spirits had been cast out, and the houses swept—and were empty.

For the second example I have chosen one that concerns an inanimate and inedible aitu. It is the case of the war god, Papo, whose considerable power was concentrated in a venerated shrine, a piece of matting that was attached like a battle flag to a war canoe going into action. At the fono (council) of this group it was determined that they destroy the shrine and put on the white cloth or armband. The shrine would either have to be burned or drowned in sea water (recognized methods both widely used throughout Oceania). The matter was debated at length by the group, which decided to tie a stone to the matting shrine, and, taking it on a new canoe (i.e., not one dedicated to war, in itself an act of desecration), throw it overboard in the deep sea. Several chiefs, Fauea among them, set off to do this so that the shrine of Papo might be visibly and ceremonially drowned.

These two incidents, in which the deities and persons involved can be identified and documented, demonstrate that the locus of power was regarded as the shrine of the god, and conversion to [the Christ-way] had to be an ocular demonstration of encounter at this point. There were, no doubt, scores of important features in the total complex, but in the final analysis decision to quit paganism and become [a Christ follower] was a dynamic demonstration on the level of [spirit reality]. This was so on the level of the individual, as it was also of the group. In the case of the group there had to be . . . discussion and agreement. . . .

Laulii, a Christian Samoan who lived nearer to those times than ours, described conversion in these terms of encounter with the aitu by saying that when any Samoan "resolved to declare himself a [Christ follower], he commenced by killing and eating" his aitu—grasshopper, centipede, octopus, bat, snake, eel, lizard, or parrot, as the case might be. I note that Laulii conceives this as an individual act. Yet it was a public act and would usually be at the family meal when the taboo creature was served up before the whole family. From evidence in other areas we would expect the family to eat the family aitu, and the individual his own personal aitu, if this distinction existed as it did in some places.

The question of what pressures might be exerted to achieve unanimity is a serious one in some communities; but in Oceania such pressures operated more against conversion than for it. Sometimes persons who agreed with the common decision were nevertheless quite frightened about the power test, as we have seen in the oil and sea water antidote incident, and this is why the

period of Christian instructional follow-up is so important. Perhaps it is true that some would be swept into the
movement with the crowd, but this was never exploited
by Protestant missionaries and they were most vocal
about its undesirability. (*People Movements*, 163–66)

As another example, Tippett refers to the experience of the
Tahitians under King Pomare II:

> The king had asked for Christian baptism in November
> 1811 but had been refused by the missionaries. He was
> deemed not ready to become a member of the church.
> Between then and July 1812, Pomare had come to realize
> that some dynamic encounter was required, not only to
> convince his fellow countrymen of the truth, but also to
> convince the missionaries of his sincerity. The missionar-
> ies kept him waiting seven years for baptism, not because
> of sincerity, but because he needed more instruction.
> Pomare had heard the Christian message and become
> convinced that Jesus was more powerful than their tra-
> ditional gods.
>
> Pomare had, for some time past, shown his con-
> tempt for the idols of his ancestors, and his desire to be
> taught a more excellent way. . . . The natives had watched
> the change in his mind with the most fearful apprehen-
> sion. . . . They were powerfully affected on one occasion
> when a present was brought to him of a turtle, which was
> always held sacred, and dressed with sacred fire within
> the precincts of the temple, part of it being invariably of-
> fered to the idol. The attendants were proceeding with
> the turtle to the [temple], when Pomare called them
> back, and told them to prepare an oven, to bake it in his
> own kitchen, and serve it up, without offering it to the
> idol. The people around . . . could hardly believe the king
> was in a state of sanity. . . . The king repeated his direc-
> tion; a fire was made, the turtle baked, and served up at
> the next repast. The people of the king's household stood,
> in mute expectation . . . of the god's anger. . . . The king
> cut the turtle and began to eat it, inviting some that sat
> at meat with him to do the same; but no-one could be
> induced to touch it . . . (1971:16).

Pomare's actions were the flowering of his hearing and believing the Christian message. In a society that feared the spirits, he risked his life by challenging the only spiritual powers they had ever known. And his people stood around waiting for the spirits to take revenge by killing him.

This was a classic power encounter and resulted in the conversion of many people, a conversion that took place in line with the people's custom. They changed allegiance to the more powerful god. And they all followed their king together.

A further example concerns a Tahitian priest named Patii who served several gods symbolized by wooden images. After a period of time when Patii was considering changing his allegiance, he decided to convert and lead his followers to change gods. So he scheduled a meeting of his followers and a large number of them gathered.

He then instructed his servants to build a fire. Then he stripped each idol, talked to it, informing it that he was no longer following it. He then ceremoniously disrobed the gods, throwing into the fire each piece of clothing and eventually the wooden idols themselves. As he did this, he pointed out to the spectators the inability of each god to resist the superior power of the true God.

Again, the people stood around, expecting the gods to take revenge by killing the priest. And many of them feared for their own lives as well. But nothing evil happened. So the people converted.

Tippett gives several additional examples. In the Solomon Islands when the people decided against their gods, they ceremonially buried their ancestral skulls, the focal points of their allegiance to the gods.

In West Irian, as the gospel message spread through the Baleim valley it became the norm to burn fetishes as the people changed allegiance. In Tonga the converts publicly desecrated and hung their idols. In Samoa a group that had been studying Christianity demonstrated their change by eating the sacred fish in a non-ceremonial way. There were no negative results.

Kinds of Power Encounters

The first kind of PE may be called Face–to-Face Confrontation. Some of these confrontations are unsought, as with the attack on Jesus in Nazareth (Luke 4:28–30). Others are open challenges, such as Elijah and the prophets of Baal (1 Kgs 18:18–40) or Moses and Pharaoh (Exod 7–12) or Gideon (Judg 7) or the South Pacific examples cited above.

When the concept is expanded to include contemporary encounters, we see representatives of the true God commanding healing and deliverance as open challenges or encounters designed to defeat the enemy. These encounters are visible challenges.

There are, in addition, quite a few types of invisible power encounters where the challenges are largely through prayer and asserting the authority given us by Jesus (John 14:12; Luke 10:17). These challenges materialize into insider spiritual battles over territories, systems, institutions, churches, schools, political organizations and the like. There are battles over territories (countries, cities, regions) issues (prostitution, homosexuality, abortion), relationships (families, friendships, work relationships), individual behavior (lying, lust, self-will), demonization (individuals, institutions, whole societies). There are even power encounters between the covenant box and God's people in the Old Testament. See 1 Sam 5:1–8 for an encounter with the god Dagon and 1 Sam 5:8–12 for encounters at Gath and Ekron.

Wherever we turn, the conflict between God's kingdom and Satan's is obvious to those who have eyes to see what's going on in the spirit realm. God reveals himself in these encounters as a God of power working within the culture.

Results of Power Encounters

The results of power encounters are mixed. Though power encounters were an important part of people movements in the South Pacific, the encounters did not always result in people movements. People did not always respond positively to the power demonstrations.

Because our Western Christianity is largely powerless, we may assume that if people see the power of God in action, they will automatically begin to follow the God who wins the encounter. We may assume that the normal response is as follows:

Power Encounter	→	Success of the Christian Witness	→	Many Believe

What we often miss is the fact that animistic peoples are used to seeing demonstrations of spiritual power. They are also used to inviting any power to help them. They're not used to going exclusively with one god or spirit. They'll accept blessings or healings from one spirit today and from another tomorrow, even if tomorrow's spirit is weaker than today's.

Short term, the power encounter may make a great impression and bring in a large number of converts. Long term, however, many people simply accept healing, blessing, or the defeat of their god and go right back to it. Note the situation recorded in Scripture where the Israelites went right back to Baal after Elijah defeated the prophets (see 1 Kgs 22:6).

Elijah	→	Demonstrates God's Power	→	Elijah Flees	+	Jezebel Appoints New Prophets, but God's Remnant Is Encouraged

Families often ostracize those who convert. In Tonga, a convert's family threw a feast for their god and ceremonially disinherited the convert. By so doing they sought to protect themselves from the anger of their family god (Tippett, *People Movements*, 97). Often there is a revolt and a return to the old gods, as with those observing the encounter between Elijah and the prophets.

One chief, however, thwarted such a return to the old gods by calling for a feast and blessing the food in the Christian manner. This disqualified the food from serving as a pagan offering.

Even those who conduct a power encounter often get discouraged. Elijah fled in fear to the wilderness. Gideon retired, went back to his village, made an idol, worshipped it and misled Israel. Often a power encounter is followed by the religious or political institution rising up to defeat God's witness. Persecution, suffering, death, and opposition result. Some believe, but the witness often suffers some negative consequences.

How Are Power Encounters Understood?

There are several meanings attached to power encounters by those who observe them. I have pointed out above that not everyone who observes a power encounter is swayed from their previous loyalty. For many animists, power demonstrations are more or less routine. Their gods compete with one another and the winners attract the most followers. But these contests between the gods and the choices made by their followers are internal to the society.

Along comes the powerful god of another society that is more powerful than the indigenous gods and the people acknowledge that superiority but may not change their allegiance. They simply recognize that the gods of another society are more powerful than their gods but often reason that their power only works within their contexts. Other spirits work in their contexts and perhaps occasionally in other contexts. But, they reason, there is not enough evidence for them to risk a change of allegiance to a god that may not be more powerful than the old, familiar god.

When the White Man's God comes into contact with the gods of an animistic society, then, he may be recognized as more powerful than the local deities in the White Man's context. But there may be no inclination for his people to convert. This may be because they make allowances for the exercise of the power of the God of the Whites, feeling that they are only eligible for the power of their own gods and ineligible to appeal to this God because he belongs to the Whites and cares for them only.

Or the power encounter may be successful (from our point of view) and the people choose to follow the God who wins the contest, usually at considerable risk of revenge by the gods they have left. We see several examples of this response in the cases given above.

When change of allegiance happens, it is a very significant event. Those who turn away from the greatest power they have ever known, do so at considerable risk. They are turning away with the expectation that their tribal god will try to kill them. Indeed, usually observers stand awaiting a kick back from their god. A primary question in their minds, then, is whether the new God will be able to protect them.

The motivation is important here. In Tippett's research he sometimes suspected that at least some of the animist kings chose to follow the new God for political reasons. In their thinking they may be attempting to gain greater power to establish their thrones.

In Hawaii, then, we are told that the animist gods had died. There was no encounter here in the sense in which we have been discussing power encounters since the gods had lost their power. The Christian God, once introduced, filled a void that had been created when the traditional gods died.

Process Leading to Power Encounter

Power encounters do not usually happen without some prior experience that alerts people to the possibility. There is usually a time of observation, and usually reports of encounters that have happened on other islands. There usually needs to be something that makes a people aware of the possibility of such an encounter. In the South Pacific, as in other places, the missionaries sometimes served this purpose. But in many cases, it was the nationals who had travelled to places experiencing power encounters who alerted a people to the possibility.

Beyond learning about power encounters, there needs to be a willingness on the part of political or religious leaders—those who have authority over a population—to challenge the powers they have worshipped and depended on. And the stakes are high. That's why such confrontations often attract a crowd who watch, expecting tragedy.

These people are well acquainted with spiritual power. They probably have experienced many power demonstrations over the years. And their experience of the power of their deities makes them very fearful of what might happen when their god(s) retaliate. They often fully expected their god to strike the challengers dead. When retaliation did not happen, then, it was a powerful statement that the God of the Christians was powerful enough to protect the challengers.

When the Christian God won the encounter, the people had to make a choice. They could either change their allegiance or ignore the results of the encounter(s). Some did ignore the significance of the encounter and continued to follow their traditional gods. They felt, as mentioned above, that they have their gods, the Whites have theirs.

There is a parallel to this situation in the Scriptures. In 1 Kgs 20:13–30 we see the Israelites at war, defeating the Aramites in engagements in the hills. The king of Aram and his counselors, then, assume that the reason why the Israelites defeated them was the fact that Israel's God is a mountain god. Therefore, if his army could entice the Israelite army down onto the plain, they could defeat them. This analysis angered and insulted God, leading him to empower the much smaller Israelite army so that they won the confrontation on the plains (even though it was the wicked king Ahab in charge of the Israelites). When the true God is in the encounter, his side wins.

The Message for Us

Jesus said we're to do what he did (John 14:12). Jesus' whole ministry was a series of power encounters. The Christianity of Jesus featured power demonstrations in abundance. With this in view, the anemic Christianity of non-charismatic churches does not look like his. I compliment charismatics and Pentecostals for including spiritual power in their approach and regret that many Pentecostals and charismatics have abandoned power ministry, often in what looks like an attempt to be seen as respectable by mainstream Christianity.

It is ironic that in these days of secular Christianity, God has called non-charismatics like Tippett (or me) to seek to restore to our faith the power dimension that was so important to Jesus. Another non-charismatic, James Kallas (a Lutheran NT scholar), points out that there are two basic themes in the Synoptics and Pauline Epistles. He labels these the "Godward View" and the "Satanward View." In these two sections of the New Testament, Kallas claims 80 percent is devoted to the Satanward View (power Christianity) and only 20 percent to the Godward View (love, forgiveness, faith, peace Christianity). Both messages are there, but the one most of Christianity neglects is the statistically most frequent one (Kallas, *Satanward View*).

I'm not prepared to accept or challenge these figures except to suggest that neglecting the majority of the NT is a serious mistake, especially if we claim that ours is a Bible-centered faith. With his keen eye for historical fact and its implications for the present, Alan Tippett has uncovered a truth the contemporary church needs to listen to.

Jesus engaged in power encounters and gave his disciples and us authority and power to cast out demons and heal (Luke 9:1–2), and to train others to do the same (Matt 28:20). His aim was to free people from the enemy (Luke 4:18–19). His method was power wrapped in love. We are to go into the world as witnesses. But, what many miss is that he told his followers not to go without power (Acts 1:8).

In addition, we are to communicate the gospel as Jesus did (Mark 16:15) and to make disciples as Jesus did (Matt 28:19). He says, as the Father sent me, so I send you (John 20:21) to do what Jesus did. The normal Christian life means doing what Jesus did— teaching, healing, blessing, forgiving and casting out demons. All of these involve spiritual power and power encounters.

Jesus' style, then, is also to be imitated. He didn't get excited or overemotional, except for his compassion. He cried on occasion out of pity or upset that people weren't paying more attention. He taught and healed with authority but was not loud. He didn't shout, for neither God nor Satan are hard of hearing. He simply, with authority, spoke things into happening, and that authority was a challenge to the Pharisees, winning their hatred and eventually bringing about his death. He also leveled an attack against Satan's power and this also figured in his death.

There is a warning here. When we get into spiritual power, we challenge spirit power as Jesus did and win opposition from both human and spirit entities. We are at war and it is a power game. We can expect wonderful victories if we engage, no victories if we continue to practice powerless Christianity. We will also meet opposition both human and spiritual, just as those in the South Pacific did. But there will be a Jesus-type Christianity if we incorporate power encounter expression in our faith.

CHAPTER 2

Power Encounters in Scripture

GOD'S CASEBOOK, THE SCRIPTURES, is full of power encounters. The exercise of power demonstrations is one of God's favorite ways of alerting humans to the fact that he is there and active in human affairs. In some of those recorded in Scripture, God's side wins. In others, God's side loses.

Our God prefers to work in partnership with us, his creatures. Whether or not God's side wins, therefore, depends on the faithfulness of his human partners. In the confrontation between Moses and Pharaoh, Moses is faithful and God's side wins. Not so, though, with Adam and Eve in the garden of Eden where Adam and Eve disobeyed. Adam, using the authority God had given them gives the victory to Satan.

Following are a number of scriptural power encounters for us to learn from.

The Woman and Her Seed: A Power Encounter Lost (Gen 3:1–15)

The enemy comes to Eve and raises questions about God's motives. He questions God, engaging in partial truths. He says, "You will not die" (Gen 3:4), which is true if the subject is human life. But God was speaking about spiritual life. Then Satan promises they will "become like God" (Gen 3:5). But they were already like God by creation (Ps 8:5). Thoroughly deceived, they disobey their partner (God), lose the power encounter and misuse their authority with eternal consequences.

There are several human predicaments highlighted in this power encounter. Adam and Eve are tempted to trust the wrong person, to seek knowledge without checking with their Partner (Gen 3:5), trusting the wrong person without checking with God (Gen 3:6). The result of this loss, then, was shame and hiding (Gen 3:7–8). They covered the physical to hide the spiritual.

There were three encounters here that we will deal with in more detail later. There's the power encounter. But there is also an allegiance encounter where they are tempted to obey someone other than their Partner. Then there is a truth encounter focusing on whether or not the statements of Satan are to be believed in place of the statements of God.

Satan uses his power to blind Adam and Eve (2 Cor 4:4). He focuses their attention on his words and his trustworthiness. He puts doubt into Adam and Eve's minds, stirs up their desire and keeps them from consulting their partner, God.

However, God does not leave them without hope. He promises both good and pain and striving. But he also promises that God's partner will crush the head of our enemy (Gen 3:15). It is to this ultimate encounter that God points when he leads the Apostle Paul to say, "The God of peace will soon crush Satan under your feet."

Birth of Moses Foreshadowing Jesus (Exod 1:1–2:10; Matt 2:1–18)

This power encounter centers around the way God partnered with a mother to rescue a baby from the Pharaoh in order that that baby, Moses, could partner with God to rescue his people from slavery in Egypt. And the story of how God worked to free Moses has a remarkable parallel in the story of how he rescued the baby Jesus from vain King Herod.

Satan doesn't know the future. He knows the past very well, however, including God's special concern for Israel. Satan is also limited in how and when he can use his power. Satan faces these time and power limitations every time he seeks to torment God's people. He can't, therefore, simply do the things he wants to do when there's too much resistance from faithful humans working with God.

Long before the events we will focus on, God and Joseph had made an agreement for Israel to occupy a part of Egypt. As long as that agreement was remembered, Israel was safe. God's protective power was in full force. But a new king came along, a king who, on the one hand, felt threatened by the Israelites and, on the other, was not inclined to honor that agreement. This provided Satan an opportunity to torment God's people (Exod 1:8).

So Satan puts fearful thoughts concerning Israel into the minds of the Egyptians (Exod 1:9, 10). And instigates plans to oppress them (Exod 1:11, 12b–14). Meanwhile, perhaps the Israelites have let their relationship with God deteriorate. Their angelic protection has lessened. Yet God enables them to multiply (Exod 1:12).

Summarizing the Encounter

A. At the Human Level

1. Satan often/always tries to kill children at birth.

2. Oppression, enslavement of the Israelites (Exod 1:13–14).

3. The king instructs the midwives to kill boy babies to lessen Israel's potential power (Exod 1:15–16).

4. But the midwives feared God and let the boys live (Exod 1:17).

5. The king asks, "Why?" and the midwives lie (Exod 1:18–19).

6. The midwives are blessed and so are the Israelites (Exod 1:20–21).

7. So the king commands the murder of all the boys (Exod 1:22).

8. But a family works out a plan (Exod 2:1–4).

9. A princess with a mother's heart partners with God (Exod 2:5–10).

B. At the Cosmic Level

1. Satan trying to destroy or at least cripple God's people.

2. Doesn't know what God's plan is. But probably sees increased angelic activity.

3. Satan focuses on reducing the potential military capability of Israel.

4. Probably doesn't even recognize the threat of the princess's rescue of Moses.

5. Whether or not he sees a threat, he can't overcome the mother heart of the princess.

6. Human will can counteract Satan's plans if used in partnership with God.

As mentioned above, there is an interesting parallel in the New Testament. These NT encounters relate to the coming of Jesus. Again, Satan doesn't know what's going on. He would surely know of the announcements of Jesus' birth. But he could see angelic protection for Jesus and family. Satan probably suspected something but was very puzzled. I doubt he understands prophecy any better than we do.

He can't work unless people allow him to. He couldn't get at Joseph, Mary, or those around them. Finally, though, Satan was able to get at Herod (Matt 2:1–18). Jesus had already been born—perhaps one to one and a half years old. The wise men call Jesus "King of the Jews" (Matt 2:2) and Herod feels threatened (Matt 2:3). Satan and Herod plan murders but fail. These were power encounters that succeeded for God though the price was high for all those whose children were killed.

Power Encounters between Moses and Pharaoh (Exod 3–12)

The power encounter that is given the most space in the OT is the series of encounters between Moses (and Aaron) on God's side and Pharaoh with his priests on Satan's. What might be considered a smaller encounter is that between God and Moses. Moses was God's choice to lead the exodus of his people from Egypt. But he made a mistake, killing an Egyptian who was oppressing an Israelite (Exod 2:12). He then ran into the wilderness and kept out of touch looking after sheep for forty years, until God won their power encounter!

But the encounter we focus on here is the one between God with Moses on the one side and the Egyptian king with the Egyptian gods and their followers. As I've noted, there is both a spiritual side and a human side to all encounters.

There was a series of events leading up to the power encounters designed to get Moses to do the job God had called him to. These constituted a kind of power encounter between God and Moses. God wanted to do something and he chose a human partner to join him in his quest. But Moses was not ready to join the program. The good news is, he changed and won the encounter. Following is the sequence of events leading to a change in Moses.

1. The people of God persecuted in Egypt, experiencing great difficulty for at least eighty years (Exod 7:7).

2. God hears their groaning (Exod 2:23–25).

3. Moses goes to Midian after running from Pharaoh (Exod 2:15–16).

4. He's taking care of Jethro's sheep.

5. He sees a bush burning but not consumed (Exod 3:2–3).

6. God speaks to him (Exod 3:4–22).

7. God says "Go to the Israelites" (Exod 13–17).

8. Go with the leaders to Pharaoh (Exod 18–22).

9. God gives Moses miraculous power (Exod 4:2–17).

The Encounters (Exod 5–13).

The encounters are with the gods of Egypt represented by the priests.

1. Makes a rod a snake and back again (Exod 7:8–12).

2. Changes water to blood (Exod 7:17–21).

3. A plague of frogs (Exod 8:1–15).

4. A plague of gnats (Exod 8:16–19).

5. Swarms of flies (Exod 8:20–32).

6. Animals die except those of Israel (Exod 9:1–8).

7. Plague of boils (Exod 9:8–12).

8. Hail—except in Goshen (Exod 13–35).

9. Plague of locusts (Exod 10:1–20).

10. Plague of darkness (Exod 10:21–29).

11. Killing of firstborn (Exod 11:1–10).

These power encounters were finally successful, though the king of Egypt demonstrated what might figure as the greatest stubbornness recorded in history.

Power Encounters as Israel Moves into the Land

The conquest of the land by Israel is a picture of the place of power encounters as the Israelites move into the land. The people of the land had squandered their right to that land by giving themselves to pagan gods and pagan practices (Deut 18:12). But these peoples were still in the land and needed to be confronted and driven out.

God tells Joshua to be strong and courageous for the Lord is with him (Josh 1:9). God's partner needed encouragement. So did the people (Josh 3:7). For they were about to challenge a river (Josh 3:14–17), then the people living in the land.

Jericho was the first obstacle they were to encounter. God gives Joshua and his people a strange instruction (Josh 6:3–5). They obey and the walls of Jericho fall. The encounter is a success.

God gives directions, the people obey, the fortress is broken through, the walls came down, the city was theirs, the encounter is a success.

The next encounter, however, did not go so well. The city of Ai should have been taken easily. But there was sin in the camp and overconfidence in the army (Josh 7:1–5). No one consulted God. If they had, they would have found out there was a spiritual problem and been able to rectify it. But they did not consult God and lost their spiritual advantage by losing an encounter with God. The human part of the partnership was crippled through not consulting God and falling into disobedience. So the power encounter with Ai was lost. So was a power encounter with God.

The basic principle is that disobedience to God empowers Satan (and his people), resulting in the losing of power encounters. In this case, the disobedience of one man (Achan) results in defeat for the whole nation. To rectify this, they consult God, find out what to do to cleanse the situation and punish Achan and his whole family (Josh 7:24–26). It is the responsibility of the leader (Joshua) to ferret out disobedience. He did this and the encounter with God is taken care of. God is satisfied (Josh 7:26b), then Ai is defeated (Josh 8:1–29). Next is an encounter with the Gibeonites who tricked them. Again, they did not consult God (Josh 9:14). So Israel lost their encounter again.

Israel apparently learned the lesson God wanted to teach them. They won encounters with the Amorites (Josh 10:1–15), five southern kings (Josh 10:16–43), the northern kings (Josh 11:1 23), the kings east of the Jordan (Josh 12:1 6), the kings west of the Jordan (Josh 12:1–8), in all thirty-one kings and their cities (Josh 12:24). So Joshua challenged the enemy at many times and in many places in a series of power encounters that enabled Israel to conquer all the land (Josh 11:16). Through these power encounters, God put the enemies in Joshua's hands (Josh 11:20).

Gideon (Judg 6-8)

The next set of power encounters in Scripture was while Gideon was Israel's leader. The Midianites were oppressing Israel (Judg 6:1–6). They cried out to God and he chose Gideon to encounter these enemies. Once again, God chooses a reluctant representative to encounter Israel's enemy and he challenges both the Midianites and their god (Judg 6:11–32). The first encounter was very like those that Tippett discovered in the South Pacific except that those Tippett discovered were aimed at the enemy. This encounter was designed to convince Gideon that God would lead him and his army to defeat the enemy (Judg 6:11–24). This encounter, then, was an experience with an angel designed to prove that God would be with Gideon in encounters with the Midianites (Judg 6:25–27). Then there was an encounter with his own people who feared a reprisal from their god (Baal) because Gideon had desecrated their altar (Judg 6:30–32). "Let Baal defend himself" were the words of Gideon's father, signifying the turning of Gideon and his family to a new god (Yahweh) (Judg 6:31–32).

These encounters were successful, leading to faith on the part of Gideon and his people. But, from God's point of view Gideon's army was too large. So God required one more "faith encounter," through which God whittled Gideon's forces down to three hundred, an impossibly small number to take on the thousands in the Midianite army. God said Gideon's army was too large because if the Israelites won with the large number they would brag about their victory (Judg 7:2–3).

Then God used a dream, then rams' horns, the breaking of jars, torches in the middle of the night and the cry "the sword of the Lord and of Gideon" to give victory in the power encounter (Judg 7:9–25). The Midianites ran or were killed—120,000 at first and many others later (Judg 8:10) and others ran and hid.

This was followed by another kind of encounter. The Israelites wanted Gideon to be their king (Judg 8:22). But he refused, went back to his home village, made an idol and his people returned to idolatry (Judg 8:22–35). Thus the power encounters that God won with and through came to nought as Israel forgot the Lord and lost what they had gained.

King Saul Loses an Encounter (1 Sam 15:10–34; 16:14–23; 18:6–16; 19:1–24)

King Saul had been close to God and was chosen by God to be the king of Israel (1 Sam 10:1). But when God told him to destroy the Amalekites he chose not to. God had sent him to eradicate a people but he kept much of their things plus the life of their king (1 Sam 15:9). Probably for spiritual reasons, God wanted the Amalekites encountered and wiped out even to their animals, allowing the spiritual corruption to remain. Then Saul lied to God concerning it (1 Sam 15:7–9).

This disobedience was very serious. The evil of the Amalekites was such that only total destruction would satisfy God. But Saul allowed the king and the best animals to live, disobeying. Probably this was not Saul's first disobedience, not the first time he had refused an encounter.

But this one was so serious that God removed his spirit from Saul and an evil spirit took over (1 Sam 16:14–23). The power encounter was lost. And Saul gives in to jealousy, anger and fear, even to the extent of trying to kill David (1 Sam 18:6–16; 19:1–24). Finally, since God no longer answers him, he goes to a servant of God's enemy, a medium (1 Sam 28:3–25), confirming that this encounter has been lost.

David: An Encounter Is Won (1 Sam 17–30; 2 Sam 11)

The next set of power encounters concern David. A giant named Goliath challenges Israel morning and evening for forty days (1 Sam 17:1–16). In this case the enemy makes the first challenge. There is no indication that Israel consulted God. They simply lived in fear, dealing with it at the human level only.

David hears the heathen's challenge and volunteers to encounter the giant. He cites his experience protecting sheep as his qualification and shows no fear.

David arms himself with a sling and five smooth stones (v. 40). Goliath approaches, curses David, is hit by one of David's stones and is killed (vv. 41–51). A power encounter is won.

David: A Failed Power Encounter (2 Sam 11)

David avoids a warfare power encounter, staying in Jerusalem while his army was at war (2 Sam 11:1). He sees Bathsheba bathing, experiences temptation, does not consult God.

He lies with her, they make love, she gets pregnant (2 Sam 11:5). He loses the encounter and makes it worse by having her husband killed in battle. The Lord was not pleased because David had misused power. There is repentance and forgiveness but there is also a penalty (2 Sam 11:25).

Elijah, the Prophets and Jezebel (1 Kgs 18–19)

There was a drought and a famine in Israel. The people were worshiping the Baal gods. The prophet Elijah prophesies that rain will come (1 Kgs 18:1–2). He then calls for Ahab to call a meeting with the prophets of Baal and orders them to assemble with 450 prophets of Baal and 400 prophets of Asherah among them (1 Kgs 18:19).

When the people had gathered, Elijah had two bulls butchered sacrificially, one on an altar dedicated to Baal, the other on an altar dedicated to Yahwah. The issue was that the people would follow the god who won the power encounter, whichever god sent fire (1 Kgs 18:24).

The priests of Baal called on their gods to consume the meat. The people prayed to Baal and danced till noon, but no fire came. They continued to dance and shout, even cutting themselves all afternoon. Elijah taunted the priests of Baal then called on the Lord and he sent fire, burning up the sacrifice, the altar and everything around, proving that he was the most powerful god, the one worthy of being followed. Seeing this, the people fell on their faces and cried out, "The Lord is God" (1 Kgs 18:25–40).

Elijah then called out to the people to catch the prophets of Baal and kill them (18:40). And rain came (1 Kgs 18:41–46).

Then Elijah had an encounter with Jezebel and runs in fear to the desert where he has still another encounter, this one with God (1 Kgs 19:9–18). The result of this encounter is that Elijah is recommissioned and then replaced by Elisha (1 Kgs 19:15–18).

Daniel: A Power Encounter in the Air (Dan 10:2— 11:2)

Daniel was living in Persia. This was enemy territory but he was faithful to God, in "mourning" for three weeks (Dan 10:2). He was fasting, humbling himself in prayer "to gain understanding" (Dan 10:12). He was met by an angel after the three weeks (Dan 10:4–10). He expects to have gotten an answer by now.

He faints but the angel lifts him up and explains the delay. God had sent the angel to answer his prayer as soon as Daniel had uttered it. But he was opposed by an enemy angel called "the angel prince of the kingdom of Persia" (Dan 10:13). It was this evil angel that had the power to delay the coming of the angel sent to answer Daniel's prayer.

One of the chief angels, Michael, the guardian angel of Israel, had been sent to free him. But there was a power encounter in the air between the angel that had been sent and the one called the Prince of Persia. And only after the angel Michael came to help win the battle was the sent angel able to win the battle in the air. Only then was the sent angel able to receive the answer.

The sent angel, then, was able to carry out his mission. But awaiting him on the way home were two power encounters, one with the guardian angel of Persia and another with the guardian angel of Greece. The good news is, though, that Michael will continue to help (Dan 10:21).

Jesus and Satan (Luke 3:21–22; 4:1–14)

As mentioned earlier, the coming of Jesus provoked a long series of power encounters between Jesus and Satan. The Son of God had entered the world innocent, with no sin nature. Though he had a divine nature as well as a human nature, he had agreed with the Father never to use it.

Satan was puzzled. He is not omniscient. He doesn't know God's plans and doesn't know the future. But he can guess that a massive power encounter is coming. Satan probably tried many times to kill Jesus but couldn't penetrate God's protection. From Jesus' early days we know only of Satan's attempt to kill Jesus soon after birth. Satan used Herod's jealousy. But Herod's plan was thwarted by God's warning to Joseph and Mary. Joseph took his family and headed for Egypt.

But when God's time had come for the power encounters that made up Jesus' ministry, God led him to join John the Baptist's faith renewal movement. Jesus comes to John asking to join the movement (Luke 3:21–22; Matt 3:13–17; Mark 1:9–11). Through baptism (an initiation ceremony) Jesus joined the renewal movement. At that point God empowered him by sending the Holy Spirit (Matt 3:16). God's voice endorsed him.

The Holy Spirit then leads Jesus into a deserted area considered to be belonging to demons, Satan's territory, (Mark 1:12). Jesus' mandate was to retake the territory (probably Israel) from the enemy. He fasted and prayed for forty days, all the while encountering the enemy in his territory. Jesus faced this as a human being. He had no divine power except the Holy Spirit.

Next come a series of power encounters (Luke 4:1–13). They parallel the encounter between Adam and Satan. The issue is obedience. Will Jesus obey God or Satan? Will he break his agreement with the Father? He is God. Will he assert his divinity? He has chosen to live totally dependent on the Father (John 5:19; Phil 2:5–8). Will he obey or rebel in these power encounters?

Satan's temptations were all prefaced with, "If you are God's Son." Jesus could have turned the stones into bread, but the Father hadn't told him to. He could have thrown himself from the temple and been rescued, but the Father hadn't told him to. He could have taken the kingdoms of the world even without worshipping Satan, but the Father hadn't told him to. Jesus chose, totally as a human being, to obey the Father. No memorized lines. No cheating. Jesus worked with human choice and the Holy Spirit alone in this power encounter.

And the Second Adam succeeded where the first had failed. I believe that in winning, Jesus also broke at least some of the territorial claims of the enemy. The rest of Jesus' life, then, was a continual series of power encounters.

Three Power Encounters in Paul's Ministry (Acts 16:16–24; 19:11–41)

I believe power encounters were as common in the New Testament as in the Old. There were individual challenges such as with the sorcerer Elymas who served Satan and lost (Acts 13:8–12). Elymas challenged God and ended up blind. Then there were the sons of Sceva (Acts 19:13–16) who apparently had some success in casting out demons. But they met a demon they couldn't handle. They engaged in a power encounter and got beat up. These were power encounters lost. Relatively few of the encounters were recorded since events induced by evil spirits were so common and people don't focus on things that everyone believes. So only the spectacular encounters were recorded. Among these were the events surrounding the interaction between Paul, Silas, and a slave girl (Acts 16:16–40).

The demonized slave girl was being used by her handlers to predict the future. The handlers made a lot of money from her predictions. She began to follow after Paul and Silas, calling out, "These men are servants of the Most High God, and they have come to tell you how to be saved" (Acts 16:17). This was the voice of a demon, apparently overwhelmed by the Holy Spirit and telling the truth.

Paul, perceiving that this was a demon, cast it out, completing the power encounter in God's favor. This, however, riled the girl's handlers since their means of earning money was now gone. This precipitated a different kind of power encounter—Paul and Silas were put in prison. Around midnight, however, there was a powerful earthquake. All the doors were opened and the prisoners could have escaped. But Paul and Silas did not escape. They stayed and guided the revival that broke out in response to the power encounters.

Another group of power encounters was performed through Paul and Silas at Ephesus (Acts 19:11–20). God was performing unusual miracles through Paul. He was even using Paul's handkerchiefs and aprons to heal and deliver. There were, however, unauthorized users of Jesus' name such as the sons of Sceva (Acts 19:14–16) who had the right formula, "In the name of Jesus, whom Paul preaches" (Acts 19:13), but no relationship to Jesus. So, the spirits responded saying, "Jesus I know, Paul I know, but who are you?" (Acts 19:15). Then the spirits attacked them and ran them off. Satan lost the power encounter. And many burned their occult books and turned to Jesus.

But this is not all. The followers of the Greek goddess "Artemis of the Ephesians" foment a riot because the converts are no longer buying their idols (Acts 19:21–41). This reverse power encounter, then, is expressed through a two-hour shouting match. The officials protected them and they got to leave unharmed.

What we have seen, then, is that what we are calling power encounter is a theme of the New Testament. We have also noted that there are several types of power encounter, some of which are no more complicated than an argument between humans. Some, however, involve the hosts of heaven. They all involve a human dimension and a spiritual dimension. Next we turn to the subject of rules and principles.

CHAPTER 3

Rules and Principles for Spiritual Power

To HELP US BETTER understand what is going on in the relationship between the human world and the spiritual world, I will here depend on a small book that David DeBord and I published in 2000. It was named *The Rules of Engagement*. In that book we tried to raise to our understanding as many as possible of the rules and principles that God has built into the universe for the relationships between human and spirit beings. These rules and principles are important to know in our attempts to understand power encounter. I am grateful to Wipf and Stock Publishers for allowing me to include here selections from that book.

There are several kinds of power in the universe. In the "natural," material or physical world we experience such things as gravity and other physical principles, the power wielded by weather, the power of germs and viruses to bring about illness, the power of poison to injure or kill and quite a number of other powers.

In the human world, then, we experience power of various kinds exercised by humans. There is, for example, the power to lead, whether achieved through political processes or by inheritance, warfare or in some other way. There is, furthermore, economic power, the power of money or other means to influence economic processes. We can also speak of power in the social arena, whether that of social status or personal prestige, whether inherited at birth or achieved through accomplishments.

There is, then, the kind of power to be focused on here, that in the spiritual world. In this realm we can speak of God's power and that of his servants, and the various levels of angelic beings. Then we can speak of the power allowed Satan and his servants, the various levels of evil spirits.

Whatever power there is, whether that of the material world, that of humans or that in the spiritual realm, God is the ultimate Source. He has supreme power over everything and everyone. But he seems to have invested the material universe with certain kinds of power (e.g., weather, gravity) and to have delegated a certain amount of power to humans (e.g., over the creation: Gen 1:26–30; over other humans: Rom 13:1–7), angelic beings (e.g., Dan 10:12–13, 21–22) and even to Satan (e.g., Job 1:6–12). And he seems to not retract that delegation of power, even when humans and satanic beings use their power to hurt. He is, however, very active both in limiting the ability of evil ones to hurt and destroy and in showering good things on the righteous (e.g., Job 1:10) and the unrighteous (e.g., Acts 14:17).

Human Perception of Spiritual Power

There are several dimensions of human perception to be considered when the subject is spiritual power. The first comes to light when we ask a question focused on in the book *Christianity with Power* (Kraft, 1989): What influence do Western worldviews have on our understandings of spiritual power?

As Westerners, we have learned that spiritual beings and powers, with the possible exception of God, are figments of overactive imaginations and, therefore, belong in the category of fairy stories. It makes for nice stories if witches can wield supernatural power to hurt people but get bested by good fairies so that the hero escapes destruction. But, we have been carefully schooled that stories that start with "once upon a time" are not to be taken seriously.

Consciously or unconsciously, then, we tend to regard the miracle stories told in church in the same way. Since many of us have not seen the kinds of supernaturalistic things we read about in the Bible, we tend to discount them except as historical (though possibly exaggerated) accounts of the kind of things Jesus, the Son of God, could do because he was God. To believe that the biblical characters who did spectacular things were just like us and that Jesus gave us power to do those same things (Luke 9:1; John 14:12) may press us beyond our limits.

Such conditioning is so deeply embedded in us that, even if we try to change our perspective and take seriously biblical and contemporary demonstrations of spiritual power, we often cannot trust our understandings. "Is it a demon or a psychological problem?" we ask. Or, "Who's to say that a given healing wasn't simply psychosomatic?" Or, "Why resort to a supernaturalistic explanation when there's a reasonably good naturalistic one?"

Meanwhile, some of us go to other parts of the world where even non-Christians seem to understand the spirit world more like it was understood by biblical peoples than like we Westerners understand it. "Do you believe in spirits?" I was asked soon after I arrived in Nigeria to serve as a missionary. I had been through seminary and, prior to that, had attended a Christian college. I had been a faithful and committed Bible student and church member in solid, evangelical churches since age twelve. I knew that Jesus dealt with evil spirits in his day but I had never encountered any myself and really didn't know how to answer that question.

I knew from my anthropological training that these people (like most of the peoples of the non-Western world) were quite focused on spiritual power. I also knew that cultural perceptions could be mistaken, both theirs and mine. Could it be that they knew more than I did in this area? I was afraid this was so. So I took their perceptions and insights seriously, but knew I had no way of discerning which of the things they told me were correct and which incorrect.

I knew we could trust scriptural perspectives. But according to whose interpretation? I knew enough not to trust Western interpretations of spiritual things, given our worldview problem. But could I trust the perceptions of the Nigerian church leaders I was working with? I never was able to solve these problems during my time in Nigeria during the late '50s.

In the early '80s, however, God began bringing into my life a large number of experiences that have seemed to me to be best interpreted in terms of the interaction between God's power and that of the enemy. Reflection on these experiences in relation to the Scriptures and a good bit of other reading has wrought major changes in my understandings and behavior with respect to the spiritual realm. Some of the fruit of these changes is apparent in these chapters.

What place should our interpretations of experience play in dealing with a topic such as this one? I have been a practitioner now for over thirty years in dealing with spiritual beings and powers. And, though there is much that I don't know, I have learned a lot in these thirty-plus years and can trust a lot of what I've experienced.

In all that follows, I take both Scripture and experience very seriously. Though we must recognize the limitations of Western perspectives, we cannot give up trying to understand simply because we know there will be problems. We must, rather, seek to recognize the problems and refuse to give up trying to understand. We must interpret both Scripture and experience as best we can, and hold tentatively what we come up with.

A Biblical Perspective on Spiritual Power

The Bible assumes power in three spheres: the spiritual, the human and the material. But in the Scriptures all three are closely interconnected. The Bible does not support our Western tendency to compartmentalize reality. We dare not, therefore, assume three quite separate spheres or entities that have little relationship with each other.

There do, however, seem to be hierarchical relationships embedded in life. The creation order shows God at the top, humans "in the image of God" second ("a little lower than God," Ps 8:5) and the material world "under our feet." Though it is not mentioned, angels and demons would be beneath humans in the hierarchy.

Two types of references, though, indicate that some sort of change has happened, presumably at the fall. First, Satan claimed a position above humans when he said to Jesus that the kingdoms of the world have "all been handed over to me," (Luke 4:6) enabling him to legitimately offer power over those kingdoms to Jesus. Second, Heb 2:6–9 (quoting Ps 8:4–6) states that Jesus in his incarnation was positioned "for a little while . . . lower than the angels" (Heb 2:9).

We theorize, then, that at the fall, Adam, who had been given power over the material world, lost his authority in that area to Satan who then became "the ruler of this world" (John 14:30; cf. 1 John 5:19), "the ruler of the spiritual powers in space, the spirit who now controls the people who disobey God" (Eph 2:2). Jesus on the cross, however, "stripped the spiritual rulers and authorities of their power" (Col 2:15), winning back for humans our rightful place immediately under God (Heb 2:8–9; Ps 8:5).

The fall resulted in humans coming under the domination of the enemy, plus a curse on nature and the snake (Gen 3). Yet from the very beginning humans have had power with God to transcend those obstacles through obedience and prayer. Such tapping into God's power by humans influences things in both the spiritual and the material realms.

We find that through obedience, wars can be won (e.g., Gideon, Joshua), healing and deliverance brought about (e.g., Elijah, Elisha, Jesus, the apostles) and weather changed (e.g., Moses, Joshua, Elijah, Jesus). Thus, spiritual power has been effectively exerted by humans in all three realms from the beginning and can be even more effectively employed now that Satan lives in defeat since the resurrection.

On the other hand, humans are subject to power exerted both in the material realm and in the spiritual realm. In the former, we are subject to gravity, seasons, day and night, weather (e.g., heat, cold, rain, storms) and the like. In relation to the spiritual realm, then, we can be protected and blessed (Job 1:10), blinded (2 Cor 4:4), healed, indwelt by and delivered from demons, oppressed

(Acts 10:38), filled with the Holy Spirit (Ac 2:4), given gifts (Heb 2:4), led (Rom 8:14) and influenced in countless other ways as well.

Things that go on in the human world have their counterparts in the spiritual world. Whether we focus on prayer to God or on yielding to the temptations of the enemy, decisions and actions at the human level trigger activity in the spiritual sphere. Throughout Scripture we see this principle illustrated. Among the many illustrations are the following: Israel's wars were fought on two levels: army versus army on earth, God versus gods in the spiritual world. In Eph 4:25–27, Paul counsels us not to lie or keep our anger, since such human behavior gives the devil a chance to influence us. Daniel's prayer (Dan 10:12) activated angelic activity in the spiritual realm.

Another type of human activity that triggers activity in the spiritual realm is blessing and cursing. The Scriptures take it for granted that words of blessing and cursing are empowered to cause the desired effects. Among the examples are the statement of God in Gen 12:2, 3 to the effect that he will bless all who bless Abraham and curse all who curse him; the blessing of Jacob on his sons (Gen 48–49) and Jesus' blessing of the disciples (Luke 24:36). In addition, blessing is attached to human obedience and cursing to disobedience in Deuteronomy 27 and 28. Similarly, blessing is attached to correct (obedient) behavior in the Beatitudes (Matt 5:3–12). When, then, cursing or persecution are directed at Christians, we are taught by Jesus and Paul to respond by blessing (Matt 5:44; Rom 12:14).

A relationship between spiritual power and the material world that occurs frequently in Scripture is shown when material objects are invested with spiritual power. The spiritual power in idols is taken quite seriously (e.g., Gen 31:19, 31–35; 35:2–4). God's power, then, inheres in a bush (Exod 3:2–4), a mountain (Exod 19:12–13), the ark of the covenant, the tabernacle and the temple. Furthermore, Jesus blesses bread (Luke 24:30) and Paul speaks of the blessing of the Communion elements (1 Cor 10:16). In Acts, then, we find handkerchiefs and aprons carrying God's power (Acts 19:12) and books carrying Satan's power (Acts 19:19).

Forms, Meanings and Empowerment

Though we should take all of this very seriously, a warning or two are in order here. Once we learn that dealing with spirit beings is not simply superstition, we need to protect ourselves against such things as a magical attitude or a tendency to condemn as satanic anything we don't happen to like. When we see healings and deliverances taking place when people use certain words, phrases and substances (e.g., anointing oil), it is easy to regard these cultural forms as magical. Likewise, when we realize that satanic beings can live in objects brought from non-Western countries, it is easy to regard all such objects that look ugly to us as infested with enemy power.

We, like all peoples, attach meanings to cultural forms on the basis of our own cultural habits. Just because God chooses to work through certain words doesn't mean that those words are magical. Likewise, just because something doesn't fit our taste it doesn't mean it is satanic. I once had a student who cut out of a textbook on the religions of the world all of the pictures she didn't like on the assumption that they were empowered.

On the other hand, there are cultural forms (e.g., words, objects, rituals) that are empowered. They may be empowered by God, Satan or by humans. But this power is not a permanent or inherent attribute of those words and things. It is something added on through dedication to the being that empowers the form. The power is derived from the personal source of the power, not from some characteristic of the word or item.

Many people, like my student, allow themselves to believe that given objects are always and automatically empowered. Many Westerners who are aware of the dangers of evil spiritual power, for example, will look at art objects or listen to music from a non-Western society and assume those things are evil in and of themselves. They are not evil unless they have been dedicated to a satanic god or spirit. The evil is in the spiritual empowerment, not in the cultural forms themselves, be they objects, words, rituals or some other cultural form.

On the other hand, many people are ignorant of the fact that artifacts from non-Western societies are often empowered. In many societies, it is customary for a craftsman to dedicate his or her production to a god or spirit. So when Westerners bring them back and keep them in their homes, they give permission to the spirit in the item to live and cause disruption in their homes. Because of this they often experience satanic interference in their lives.

The major problem in this area is that people attach meanings to cultural forms. If the forms are those of our own culture, we attach the appropriate meanings easily, on the basis of what we have learned while growing up in our own society. If, however, we encounter someone else's cultural forms, we are likely to attach the wrong meanings, either because we attached the meaning that form would have had if it was a part of our culture, or because we attached a negative meaning to something we didn't like or a positive meaning to something we did like. Just because we do or don't like something does not prove, though, that that thing is good or evil.

We need, then, to understand the relationships between cultural forms, their meanings and the potential they have of being empowered by God or Satan. Most language, most objects, most events seem to be free from supernatural empowerment, though they are often empowered by humans for purely human purposes. Human empowerment is, I believe, the result of such things as status, communicational ability and other power differentials in human relationships.

But words, objects and events can also be empowered by supernatural powers: God or Satan. When something is dedicated to God or Satan it is empowered. Empowerment is attached to words spoken in the authority of either, objects dedicated to either and rituals done in the name of either. When God or Satan has control of someone or something, that person or thing is empowered. People may be filled with the Holy Spirit and thus empowered by God. They can also be demonized and empowered by Satan.

In the Scriptures, the meat sold in the markets and the special days mentioned in Romans 14, 1 Corinthians 8, and 1 Cor

10:25–29 were apparently not empowered. Paul sees no real problem in eating that meat unless it offends someone at the meaning level. Then it is to be refused (1 Cor 10:28–33). But the sacrifices offered to demons on pagan altars mentioned in 1 Cor 10:19–21 were another matter. These sacrifices were dedicated to the enemy and, therefore, satanically empowered. The reason for not eating that meat was quite a different one.

In addition, Christians need to be very careful not to treat lightly something that is dedicated to our Lord. The table of the Lord carries both empowerment, since it is blessed, and great meaning since it is symbolic. Paul, therefore, speaks of the great importance for us of being pure in our motivation when we participate with God in the Communion service (1 Cor 11:26–32), lest evil (a curse?) happen to us.

With respect to most customs, there is no problem to Christians as long as there is only human empowerment. If one suspects there is evil empowerment, however, we should use our authority in Christ to break any satanic empowerment that might be present.

CHAPTER 4

Spiritual Principles and Rules:
The Backdrop of the Battle

Even before time began, a cosmic drama had already played itself out in the heavenlies, establishing the spiritual forces that would vie for human allegiance. The biblical record of Isaiah 14 paints the heavenly picture. Lucifer, the archangel, had stood at the right hand of God, exercising the full authority of the Father in the affairs of the creation. Lucifer's power and authority were only exceeded by that of the Creator himself. But Isaiah's story accounts a violent rending of the relationship between Lucifer and the Father. Isaiah says Lucifer's desire was "to climb up to heaven and to place his throne above the highest stars . . . where he would sit like a king . . . he would be like God" (Isa 14:13–14). What Isaiah doesn't tell us is what triggered this reaction in Lucifer. Whatever it was, the result was Lucifer's expulsion from heaven along with a significant number of angels, who chose to follow his lead. Something had obviously gone wrong in paradise.

God's Plan: Man's Dominion

A clue to the cause of Lucifer's rebellion may be found in Ps 8:5, where the psalmist records that God created man "a little lower than God himself." While historically most translators record here that man was created "a little lower than the angels," this seems to be a translation rooted more in a preconceived and historical theological mindset than linguistics. The more accurate translation suggests that in creation order, humans were placed above the angels, including Satan. It is, therefore, plausible to consider that the root of Lucifer's rebellion was that his honored place closest to God was, by God's own design, usurped by the new beings—hence the jealous and destructive rebellion that followed. This displacement would also explain Lucifer's avowed hatred of humans. The stated purpose of Satan's rule then became the destruction of God's creation, and especially the destruction of human beings as the central object of God's love in creation.

By God's plan, humankind was to have dominion over all the created order (Gen 1:28). But men and women were also created to be in intimate relationship with the Father, to "walk with him in the cool of the evening." God had placed only one requirement on humans in return for their place of dominion over the earth. They must obey the rules God set in place. The one rule mentioned in Genesis 2 was that Adam and Eve not eat of the Tree of the Knowledge of Good and Evil planted in the garden. The punishment for disobedience was death (Gen 2:17), not literal death, but "relational death" due to a separation from the Father and loss of dominion over creation.

Unfortunately, Adam and Eve didn't grasp the seriousness of their decision to disobey. Like all sin, it was a loss that had to be experienced before the larger result would be known—a result Satan knew, but wisely hid as he orchestrated the temptation. Hence, Satan's strategy in the garden became the subversion of God's plan—to seize for himself what God had given to humankind as a gift.

Satan's Plan: Dominion by Deceit

The tempter came in skillfully, looking for the weakness in humankind's defense. Not willing to reveal his stake in the deal, he focused on an attractive deception that would lead the first humans to believe they were unjustly being denied something great. The enemy still presents sin in this way. Doubt was his weapon of choice this time: he simply questioned God's motives in requiring specific obedience. "You will not surely die," he said and the seed of doubt was sown. Then he dangled the carrot, "You will be like God and know what is good and what is bad." "You will be like God . . ." (Gen 3:4). Why would those who have everything want more? Isn't it curious the way temptation always seems to appear at the exact point of our weakness?

"Created a little lower than God. . . ." Yet Adam squandered our position in creation. Temptation came. Adam disobeyed. God exposed his sin. Punishment had to be swift. "Death" came in the form of expulsion from the garden where our ancestors had complete dominion. In Adam's disobedience, we went from owning everything to owning nothing, from a life of no effort, to a life of sweat, toil and pain. Because of sin, from now on men would have to sweat for their daily bread and women would have pain in childbirth and have strife with men.

Then the real tragedy of his sin emerged; the part Darkness had kept secret. Not only did humans fall from their place of dominion, all creation fell with them. That which was hidden was then revealed. Into our vacated position of dominion came the tempter, Lucifer, now named Satan.

What had been created "good"—God's creation—now became cursed and dominated by Satan. And sin would be henceforth a part of every man's spiritual inheritance. What had not been revealed previously was the high stakes that were on the table. Now Satan would be legitimately able to say to Jesus later, "It has all been handed over to me" (Luke 4:6). God trusted Adam. But Adam failed the character test. And God lost his creation to Satan. The one who had wanted a throne for himself, now had it. The earth was his and all that dwelt therein . . . at least for a season.

Satan's Kingdom: The Rule of Evil

Having claimed the spoils of his victory, Satan set himself up as the lord of this earthly kingdom. Scripture calls him by various titles:

"the evil god of this world" (2 Cor 4:4), "the ruler of this world" (John 14:30), "the rule of the Evil One" (1 John 5:19). While he had gained his position by deceit, he ruled as if by divine right. But it must be noted that while Satan ascended his new throne and claimed his new title, he was powerless in and of himself. The power Satan exercised had originated from God the Father.

Originally Satan's power and authority came from God in his position as archangel. For reasons only God knows he allowed Satan to retain his power when he rebelled and was thrown out of heaven. But there was another distressing piece of information the deceiver knew, yet did not reveal until forced to do so. One day the Messiah, the Chosen One of God, would come to reclaim the creation and restore it and humankind to the Father (Gen 3:15). Jesus would come one day and reestablish humanity to its rightful place of dominion over the earth. Satan didn't know when this time would be, but it was an inevitability for which he must prepare. If Adam could be deceived, perhaps the Messiah could also. In the meantime, there was work to be done. If he couldn't keep his position as lord of the earth, he would then destroy as much of it as he could, along with those that inhabited it.

To accomplish his task, Satan organized his kingdom of "dark angels" into a hierarchy of authority. Since he is not omnipresent like God, he needed a chain of command to carry out his strategies. Ephesians 6:12 suggests several layers of evil, wicked forces serving under Satan's command, doing his bidding. Some believe that Rev 12:4 indicates that one third of God's angels followed Satan out of heaven. Only God knows what that number literally is, how much power Satan actually has and what its limits are. Based on the damage done in the name of evil, the amount of power and the number of demons serving him must be substantial.

God's Kingdom: The Rule of Love

"In the fullness of time, Jesus came," reports the Apostle Luke in his gospel account of the birth of Jesus (Luke 2:6). This powerful statement ushers in God's intent to redeem his creation from the clutches of the evil one. It boldly declares that even while God was allowing Satan to set up his power base in the created order, he had a plan already in place to retake it from the enemy. This declaration, "in the fullness of time," declares that when the divine time was right, when the Father had everything in place that needed to be in place, he would launch his counter-offensive on earth and in the heavenlies. He did this in the person of Jesus Christ, his Son, the Messiah, who came to earth to demonstrate the Father's love to a disenfranchised humankind.

In the coming of Jesus to earth, the kingdom of God was ushered into human history. The kingdom of God meant the reign and rule of God in the hearts of humankind was now present. It was to be our weapon in the war to retake creation. Insights into the kingdom of God, what it looked and acted like, filled the teachings of Jesus. He demonstrated it, illustrated it and commanded his disciples to live it in their lives. At his resurrection, he released the kingdom of God to his disciples, commanding them to spread it around the world.

The kingdom and its participants were empowered by the Holy Spirit the same way that Jesus was empowered by the Holy Spirit at his baptism. With kingdom power in hand, embodied in the Holy Spirit, Jesus' disciples were empowered to take on the enemy first hand and do the things that Jesus did to defeat him. Jesus' prediction to his own disciples was directive and inclusive: "Everything you saw me do you will do and more" (John 14:12).

Two Kingdoms in Conflict:
The Ongoing Power Encounter

Having identified the two sides in the battle, the war now rages—over us in the heavenlies, around us in the natural, and inside us in our bodies, souls and spirits—all simultaneously. On one side the forces of evil stand poised, intent on retaining the rule of this world and the reign of darkness. On the other side stand those with allegiance to the kingdom of God and its Savior. While Satan relies on his army of fallen angels to deceive people into accomplishing his destructive purposes, God chooses to indwell and trust human beings, the very ones who created this problem in the first place. Surprisingly, for reasons only he knows, it is a valued part of God's strategy for humans to play a vital role in re-establishing his kingdom in creation. With Jesus as our model, we have seen demonstrated the power available to us. Just as Jesus, the Second Adam, warred with Satan while on earth, so we also are to war with Satan in continuous power encounters. And our power is the same power that Jesus relied on—the power coming from the infilling of the Holy Spirit.

This was the powerful kingdom secret that Jesus demonstrated but that most believers have never known. The kingdom power demonstrated by Jesus was not found in his divinity, but in obedience—that same obedience squandered in the garden, resulting in sin. In obedience, Jesus put his divinity aside when he came in human flesh. That is why he did no public miracles until after his baptism/initiation by John the Baptist. During that public initiation done in obedience to the Father's will, the Holy Spirit came upon him. Only then did Jesus enter the power encounter to retake creation.

What Jesus did he had to do without his divinity. Otherwise, how could his followers be expected to do the same things he did? They certainly had no divinity in themselves. Therefore, Jesus had to call them, teach them and train them. And just as he had not entered encounters till power came on him, he told them at his ascension to not do anything until the gift of the Holy Spirit had been imparted to them also. Only after that happened (Acts 1:8) did the battle begin in earnest.

The battle between the kingdom of God and the kingdom of Satan still rages. Though defeated at the cross, Satan and his army of fallen angels refuse to admit defeat and are fighting to retain control of the creation through seeking and holding onto the hearts and minds of humankind. But the soldiers of the kingdom of God march under the mandate of the Savior: "to bring good news to the poor . . . proclaim liberty to the captives . . . recovery of sight to the blind . . . to free the oppressed . . . and announce that the time has come when the Lord will save his people" (Luke 4:18–19).

Our Battle Strategy: Offensive and Defensive

As soldiers of the kingdom of God our battle strategy is both defensive and offensive. It is defensive in that we are to be prepared for war, not a war such as the world fights, but a spiritual war; not against flesh and blood, but against wicked demonic beings in space (Eph 2:2; 6:12). We are called "to put on the whole armor of God" (Eph 6:10–20). We are to protect ourselves, using all the authority that the Father has given us. But the battle is also offensive; we are to be looking for "captives" to set free—captives being those who are trapped in Satan's deception, trapped by their allegiance to the darkness. Whether they are in darkness by their own choices or for lack of light, Jesus calls us to set them free, to bring light to the darkness.

It is to this battle that we now turn our attention. The portion of the battle that is most crucial to know and understand is the rules that seem to govern it. More specifically, we need to know and understand the rules that govern the spirit beings who fight with us, the angels of the kingdom of God, and the spirit beings warring against us, the dark angels of Satan's army. It appears that the same rules and principles govern both sides. Therefore, if we are to be victorious, we must begin to discover what the rules of engagement are in the battle that consumes us. The demonic spirits we battle certainly know what the rules are and use them to their advantage against us. And for us, unfortunately, ignorance of the rules or even of the battle that is raging against us does not protect us from its results.

Given that we are at war, we need to attempt to figure out some of the regularities that exist in the spirit world. Though dealing with all of the principles and rules would be impossible even if we knew them, I will attempt here to list some of the principles and to suggest some of the rules that spin off from these principles.

CHAPTER 5

Spiritual Principles

Principle 1: God Has Built Rules into the Spiritual Sphere

THESE RULES ARE JUST as firm as the rules he has put in the material and human spheres. Indeed, God himself abides by these rules, seldom, if ever, breaking them. It is, therefore, just as possible to develop a scientific study of spirit world regularities as it is of the rules by which the material and human universes operate. As there are sciences dealing with the material and human worlds, so there can be one dealing with the spiritual world.

A science is the study of regularities. The so-called law of gravity is such a regularity in the material world, as are the rest of the "laws" of physics, including the laws of aeronautics. These laws or rules affect everyone, whether or not we know or believe in them. So it is with the regularities and rules in the spiritual area. The fact that most of us Westerners are quite ignorant of these regularities and rules does not mean that they do not affect us. We are just as subject to them as we are to the law of gravity.

Principle 2: There Are Two (Actually Three) Sources of Spiritual Power

Though we have said above that there are three sources of spiritual power, God, Satan and humans, we will ignore the human source under this principle. As noted above, however, all power of any kind comes ultimately from God, even that of Satan and humans who use it to fight God. It appears that Satan was one of the highest archangels (perhaps the highest). As such, he would have been delegated a great amount of power and authority. Probably, under the rules of the universe, that power and authority is still his, neither taken away from him by God nor denied to him even though he now uses it to attack rather than to serve God.

Rule 2.1: The two sources in focus here, God and Satan, are unequal.

Christianity does not allow for a duality of equal powers, as do certain other faiths (e.g., Zoroastrianism). Though we talk of two kingdoms headed by two kings, there is not equality between the two and no chance that the satanic kingdom will emerge victorious overall—though Satan does win some battles. The power of God is infinitely greater than that of Satan. Furthermore, Satan has been miserably defeated at the cross and the grave. This defeat is symbolized, according to Paul, by the fact that Satan and his followers have been "made a public spectacle" and led "as captives in [Jesus'] victory procession" (Col 2:15).

Rule 2.2: There are spirit beings, arranged hierarchically, that serve God (archangels, cherubim, angels) and that serve Satan (principalities, powers, dark angels, demons). They are obedient to their masters (Ps 103:20; 1 Pet 3:22).

These beings have different ranks and, therefore, different power. They have names that relate to their ranks, such as archangels, prince (Dan 10:13), principalities (rulers), powers (authorities), rulers (cosmic powers) (Eph 6:12), demons.

Angelic knowledge is limited (1 Pet 1:12). The New Testament portrays angels as very interested in what humans are doing but not knowing what will happen (e.g., Matt 24:36; Luke 15:10; 1 Tim 5:21). Neither Satan nor demons know the future. Fortune-telling and other predictive activities of those who serve Satan are based on knowledge of the past coupled with guessing and cursing of the future.

Angels are sterile. Neither Satan's dark angels nor God's angels can create or reproduce (Matt 22:30). They can only work on things already there. Because they are unable to create while humans can create, at least Satan's angels are jealous of humans. Probably God's angels are also.

This rule means that if, for example, a car is in good repair, or a person is healthy (physically or emotionally), demons cannot cause a mechanical failure or physical/emotional problem and thereby bring about an accident or illness. If there is a mechanical or personal weakness, however, they may make use of it to cause an accident or illness unless a greater power is protecting it.

I once had to walk off the platform during an address I was giving to a group of pastors. The reason was a kidney stone attack that I'm sure the enemy had a hand in. He had capitalized on a physical weakness I didn't even know I had. Since then I've claimed protection from such attacks and haven't had any. I don't know when God protects us and when he doesn't, but the fact that I claim his protection may be the reason why it hasn't happened again. Or it may not be. I doubt that claiming protection would protect my car (or my body) from problems if I was careless and did not get a known problem repaired, however.

Rule 2.3: Angels, including Satan, are below humans in the created order (Ps 8:5, correctly translated).

We even get to judge them (1 Cor 6:3). Only humans, not angels, are in God's image. Only humans, not angels, can reproduce others in God's image. Only humans, not angels, are beings adequate for God to unite with in Jesus. When Adam fell, however, humans descended to a place lower than Satan and his angels so that it is said of Jesus that he came to live "for a little while lower than the angels" (Heb 2:7). From this position, then, Jesus as the Second Adam (1 Cor 15:45–47) won back our right to be a little lower than God himself (Ps 8:5).

Rule 2.4: Satan received power over creation from Adam.

In Luke 4:6, while Satan was tempting Jesus, he made the statement, "[the power and wealth of the world] has all been handed over to me, and I can give it to anyone I choose." In the beginning, God gave Adam dominion over the earth and all that was in it. When Adam fell, however, that dominion passed to Satan. Though it has been won back by the Second Adam, we have not yet seen that victory consummated.

Rule 2.5: It is clear from Scripture that spirit beings are very active and influential in the human arena.

There are, however, rules governing such activity and influence. Many of these are pointed out here. The primary rule is that they act on behalf of whichever master they serve. Dark angels, for example, are the agents of whatever their master seeks to accomplish. They, therefore, are assigned to tempt, disrupt, harass, destroy and kill. God's angels, on the other hand, are assigned to protect (Matt 18:10), perhaps to govern (Rev 1–3), to convey messages (Gen 22:11–12; Num 22:31–35; Dan 10:13) and to do whatever else God assigns them to do.

Demons can only live in humans if they have a legal right. They could not get Jesus because they could find nothing in him (John 14:30). When there is nothing there, the agents of Satan's power are like birds that cannot land (Prov 26:2).

Rule 2.6: Satan can gain permission from God to do more than he is ordinarily able to do.

We know this from the book of Job where Satan requested that God give him the right to take everything away from Job and it was granted (Job 1:9–12). Whatever power Satan had before this permission was granted, it did not extend to harming Job. After receiving permission, though, Satan had the power to destroy Job's possessions, kill his family and eventually to harm his body—anything short of killing Job (1:13—2:7).

Rule 2.7: Satan can hinder God's workings.

In Daniel 10, we have the amazing story of a prayer of Daniel's that the Lord answered immediately by sending an angel to deliver the answer. The angel was, however, blocked by a high-level spirit being called the "Prince of Persia" and had to go get the archangel Michael to enable him to break through that prince's power to get to Daniel. This process took three weeks (Dan 10:12–13). We don't know how often such hindering happens but I suspect it happens often. If God always got his way, as some theologies contend, everyone would be saved (2 Pet 3:9) and Jesus would not have had to pray, "May your Kingdom come; may your will be done on earth as it is in heaven" (Matt 6:10).

Principle 3: There Is a Very Close Relationship between the Spiritual and the Human Realms

Throughout Scripture we see this principle at work. As mentioned above, wars are fought on both levels and angelic activity is frequent. In addition, it is clear that whenever humans are faithful, God blesses, while unfaithfulness allows Satan to gain the upper hand. Likewise, when those serving God are able to work in his power while Satan's servants are able to use satanic power. Prayer, then, by humans enables God to change many things on earth.

A different kind of example of this close relationship is seen in the names of the satanic princes mentioned in Dan 10. Their authority was over Persia and Greece, human geographical entities. Whether on God's side or on Satan's, what humans do seems to affect what happens in the spirit world, and vice versa.

Rule 3.1: Any analysis of the cause of a given event in the human sphere needs to take account of both human and spiritual dimensions of the event.

When, for example, negative things such as arguments, accidents and wars or positive things such as revivals, healings and healthy relationships are analyzed only on the human level, the analysis is incomplete. Though the human motivations, decisions and actions are crucial to understanding the event, so are the activities of invisible spirit beings.

Rule 3.2: The rules for relating to the spirit world seem to be essentially the same both on God's and Satan's sides.

Though it is difficult for many of us to handle theologically, it appears that God has limited himself in major ways to the spiritual rules he has made. Though, as we will see under principle 4 below, there are significant differences in the ways in which God and Satan carry out their interactions with humans, most of the basic rules and principles seem to be the same.

For example, allegiance and obedience are the key elements enabling either power to work with and through human beings. On the basis of such allegiance and obedience, either power provides his devotees such things as protection and empowerment to serve the purposes of his kingdom. In addition, such activities as dedication, blessing, prayer, sacrifices, rituals (e.g., the Communion service) and worship dedicated to the power to whom allegiance is given produce the same effects on either side. These activities enable the power to carry out his plans on earth. Most of the principles and rules detailed below further illustrate this rule.

Rule 3.3: A very important rule that God has put into the universe is the interdependence rule that says, human allegiance and obedience give the spirit power the right to work in human affairs.

Spirit beings are enabled/empowered or disenabled/disempowered in major ways through the choices made by humans. Though allegiance/commitment to the spirit power starts this process, continued obedience is the thing that keeps the process going. When God wants to do something in the human realm, it appears that he usually needs the obedience of a human to be able to do it. As long as Adam obeyed God, he could work his will in Adam's life without hindrance. When, then, Adam obeyed Satan, Satan was empowered to take dominion over the world that had been given to Adam (Luke 4:6).

The obedience of Noah enabled God to rescue a remnant at the time of the flood. The obedience of Abraham enabled the Lord to raise up a people that would (hopefully) be faithful to him. Abraham had a choice between following the gods of his father or obeying the true God. On the basis of his choice to obey Yahweh followed by continual choices to obey (including even the willingness to sacrifice Isaac), then, God could do great things through him. When Abraham's descendants obeyed, God was able to do mighty things through them. When they disobeyed (= obeyed Satan), however, God's hands were tied.

This principle shows up constantly throughout the Bible. On the enemy's side, it took some time for Satan to get a Pharaoh who would obey him by harassing Israel. When, however, a Pharaoh came to the throne who did not honor the agreement made with Joseph (Exod 1:8), Satan was able to get that king to carry out his plan. Through a family who was faithful to him, plus an Egyptian princess who disobeyed both Pharaoh and the gods of Egypt and unconsciously obeyed God, however, God was able to raise up and train Moses to rescue his people. A similar thing occurred shortly after Jesus' birth when Satan was able to get Herod to work with him to kill the boy babies in hopes of killing Jesus (Matt 2:16). Through listening to God and obeying him, however, Joseph and Mary were able to save Jesus (Matt 2:13–15).

When, as with each of these who was faithful to God and supremely in Jesus, a person is tempted but refuses to go along with Satan, what the latter tries to accomplish does not happen. If a person is tempted by a demon to commit suicide but does not carry out the act, it cannot happen. A spirit cannot cause suicide without the person's agreement. Likewise, when God seeks to enter a person's life, it won't happen until the person invites him to come in. When, furthermore, people don't obey God by praying and witnessing, people are lost, in spite of the fact that it is not God's will that any should be lost (2 Pet 3:9). When, though, God's people obey by praying, repenting and turning away from evil, God has promised to forgive and bring revival (2 Chr 7:14).

There are probably limitations to this rule (as well as to all others listed here), but the close connection between what the spirit power wants to do and what the humans involved choose should be clear.

Rule 3.4: Commitment or dedication of a person to either God or Satan in one generation carries down to that person's descendants.

If, for example, the head of a family dedicates his family to a false god as is often done by Freemasons, Chinese, Japanese, Africans and others, the entrance of satanic power thus incurred is passed on to the following generations. Likewise, if a curse is put on a family or its head. In this way many children come into the world already demonized. There is a mystical relationship between members of the same family that means that children participate in commitments made by their parents.

Thus we see God keeping his commitments to Abraham for many generations even after Israel ceased to be faithful to him (e.g., Gideon). Likewise, with the curses uttered in the garden of Eden: they have affected every person born since that time. I don't know how many generations before such flow of spiritual power runs out. The Ten Commandments mention three to four on the enemy's side and thousands on God's, but each is conditional (Exod 20:5–6). I have often dealt with demons that claim to have been in a family for more than ten generations. I have also cast out many occult demons whose claim to the person stems from a grandfather or even farther back.

Rule 3.5: The rights given by people to spirit powers extend to their property and territory.

We see this rule enacted first when Adam sinned. That sin resulted in a curse on the land and its productivity (Gen 3:17–19) as well as the right of Satan to claim ownership of the whole world (Luke 4:6). Pagan temples (including those of false religions, Masonic temples and Mormon temples), shrines, occult bookstores and even the homes of those committed to Satan are often invested with tangible evidence of the rights the enemy has to them. Those sensitive to spiritual things often feel the enemy's presence in such places.

On occasion I have been asked to spiritually "clean out" homes and rooms over which Satan has some power due to dedication and/or sin. A demon I once cast out of a woman claimed the right to inhabit her because she lived in a house in which a previous occupant had committed adultery. Only when we claimed her authority as the new owner of the property to break his power were we able to cast him out. I have dealt with other demons who had rights to homes through occult activity, death that occurred in the home and infestation due to major sin that had been committed in a church.

When people serve God, their possessions are blessed and the houses and lands in which they live participate in that blessing. In 2 Chr 7:14, one of the blessings specified is that the land will be made prosperous again. God, of course, has rights to churches that are dedicated to him and used regularly in obedience to him.

Rule 3.6: The relationship between the spirit power and humans is fed by obedience.

As indicated above, obedience is a crucial element in giving rights to the spirit being. It is just as important in continuing those rights. When, therefore, a person is disobedient either to God or to Satan, the rights are weakened, though not broken.

For example, when one who has pledged allegiance to God sins (= disobeys God), the enemy gains an opportunity to lessen that person's closeness to God and effectiveness in serving God. In the case of those in spiritual or civic authority over others, their disobedience to God affects the whole group over which they have authority (e.g., Israel's kings). In the case of Achan (Josh 7), the sin of one apparently not in leadership affected the relationship of the whole nation to the Lord. Many evangelical churches in our day are spiritually hindered by the fact that some of their members belong to Freemasonry or are living in sexual or other sin.

When those who have committed themselves to Satan in occult organizations such as New Age or Freemasonry convert to Christ, their relationship to Satan is damaged but not broken. The demons they have let in while active in such organizations still live within them and exercise considerable influence. Complete freedom in Christ does not come until they are cast out.

On the positive side, the more devotees practice obedience, the closer their relationship grows. As Jesus said, "If you love me, you will obey my commands" (John 14:15) and, "If you obey my commands, you will remain in my love" (John 15:10). Obedience brings and maintains closeness.

Principle 4: There Are Authority and Empowerment Rules Based on Allegiance to and Relationship with God or Satan

Both God and Satan are able to grant authority and empowerment to their devotees, and through them the empowerment of places and things. Jesus gave his disciples authority and power over all demons and diseases (Luke 9:1) while he was on earth. Then, as he left the earth, he sent the Holy Spirit to empower his followers after his ascension (Acts 1:4–8) to do the works he did, and more (John 14:12). Satan also empowers his followers to heal and do other miraculous things. Such authority and power are received and maintained on the basis of the allegiance and obedience given by humans to their leader.

Rule 4.1: God and Satan can empower people, places and things.

People can receive the authority to use the power of God or Satan through committing themselves to that power and remaining in good relationship with him. Through such obedience, people get to cooperate with their power source in the carrying out of their plans, including power encounters. When people commit themselves to their power source they get to be inhabited by either the Holy Spirit or demons and are thereby invested with spiritual power from that source.

Dedication of people to given spirits gives those spirit beings authority over them. Submission and faithful obedience to whichever spirits live within given people, then, give them delegated authority under the control of that spirit. With the Holy Spirit within us, Christians carry the authority and power of God himself. The amount of authority and power available to persons on Satan's side depends on the rank of the inhabiting demons. Higher ranking demons can give a person power to do signs and wonders, as with Elymas (Acts 13:8–10) and the demonized girl of Acts 16 (Acts 16:16), even to move around out of body as in astral projection.

Places and things, then, can be empowered through being dedicated to God or Satan and/or through frequent use in the service of that power. They can also be empowered through being blessed with the power of God or the power of Satan. Scriptural illustrations include the ark of the covenant, the temple, Jesus' garment (Matt 9:20), Paul's handkerchiefs and aprons (Acts 19:12) and perhaps Peter's shadow (Acts 5:15). In contemporary life, through dedication and blessing we can empower such things as churches, homes, automobiles, anointing oil, the Communion elements, food, water and other things that pertain to us.

Rule 4.2: To work in the human realm, God or Satan need the cooperation of humans.

This rule focuses on the limitations for God or Satan if the persons they attempt to influence don't cooperate. Though there are probably limitations to this rule, it seems clear that much of what God and Satan would like to do in the human realm does not get done because there are not humans to cooperate with them. God, for example, does not want anyone to go to hell (2 Pet 3:9). But, apparently, many will. Over and over again we see things that God desires to have done such as evangelism, healing, freeing from demons, church planting and the like that don't get done because God's people do not cooperate. Undoubtedly, the same is true of Satan's kingdom. How frustrated he must be when he cannot find someone to do his will as during the years before he found a Pharaoh who felt no obligation to honor the promises made to Israel during Joseph's day (Exod 1:8).

Rule 4.3: The spirit world works within the human world according to authority relationships.

When, for example, a parent dedicates a child to either God or Satan, the spirit power has major ability to work in and with that child. Likewise with cult groups in which the members give authority over themselves to a leader. When parents give authority over their children to a babysitter, the latter can use that authority to commit a child to whatever spiritual power they serve. I have had to cast demons out of people who received them through such exercise of authority by a babysitter. On the other side, I have been involved in spiritually cleaning out homes and breaking satanic power over children when owners/parents have granted me their authority to do so.

The Scriptures point to the authority of a husband over his wife (Eph 5:23; 1 Tim 2:11–14), of parents over children (Eph 6:1–3; Col 3:20), of pastors and other leaders over the people in their churches (Eph 4:11–12; 1 Tim 3), of rulers over their people (1 Tim 2:2; Rom 13:1–2) and, I believe, of older people over younger ones. An additional authority seems to be implied in 1 Cor 7:14 of a believing parent to make the unbelieving spouse and their children acceptable to God. In dealing with demons, we find that they take these authority relationships very seriously. I assume that God does also.

Rule 4.4: Humans can be inhabited either by God's Spirit or by demons or both.

Commitment and authority rules play important parts here. That is, when people or those in authority over them invite either God or Satan to enter, they get what is asked for. Such commitments to Satan and/or wallowing in sinful attitudes provide the landing places (Prov 26:2) for satanic beings. Obedience to God, repentance and righteousness, however, bring cleansing (though not necessarily deliverance from demons) to those committed to God so that with us, as with Jesus, the enemy can find nothing in us (John 14:30).

Rule 4.5: It appears that we can enable/empower our spirit power source through the things we do.

God and Satan seem to gain more ability to do their will on the human scene when people obey them. On God's side, obedience to his rules, including such things as committing ourselves to Christ, praying, worshiping, doing righteousness, confessing sin and the like. These enable God to do what he seeks to do both within and through us. Disobedience to God, however, is obedience to Satan and enables him to do what he desires on the human scene.

Rituals, such as worship seem to especially enable God or Satan. When God is worshiped, enemy forces have to stand back and cannot carry out their purposes. When, on the other hand, worship is rendered to Satan, the forces of God have to stand back, though since God is more powerful, those who in God's power challenge the enemy usually win. Again, obedience to the spirit power on the part of humans seems to be the key ingredient. When we obey God by praying, worshiping, fasting, living faithfully by his commands and the like, he is enabled to do what he wants to do in and through us. The same seems to be the case on the other side.

In this regard, there seem to be a hierarchy of rituals. Perhaps prayer would be at or near the lower level, with blood sacrifice near the highest. On both sides of the fence, the shedding of blood seems to bring the greatest empowerment. In Old Testament times, of course, the dedication of animals in the sacrificial system provided for this. The sacrifice of Jesus, then, being the most powerful of all sacrifices, has had cosmic consequences. Perhaps the highest blood sacrifice the enemy could muster is recorded in 2 Kgs 3:21-27 when the King of Moab, on the verge of being badly defeated by the Israelites, sacrificed his oldest son to his god on the city wall (2 Kgs 3:27). Though the Israelites were winning the battle, the spiritual power inherent in this sacrificial act was sufficient to rout them. They did not seem to know enough to claim the greater power they had from their God.

Having said this concerning blood rituals, the importance and power of prayer needs to be emphasized (both under this rule and under several of those that follow). Prayer is the most easily utilized ritual and the one most frequently practiced throughout Scripture. Jesus regularly prayed and commanded his followers to do the same. As I have written elsewhere (*Deep Wounds, Deep Healing*, 237–40), however, there are at least six types of prayer, all of which are important in enabling God to do what he wants to do. All six are probably effectively utilized by the servants of Satan as well.

These types of prayer I have labeled intimacy, petition, gratitude, confession, intercession, and taking authority. Gratitude and confession praying are foundational to petition and intercession while intimacy with God is basic to all of these and especially to taking authority. The latter, then, is what we are to do when we cooperate with God in doing his work. Jesus modeled each type except confession prayer. Most noticeable in his ministry, however, were his intimacy with the Father and the authority he took in ministry on the basis of what he heard from the Father (John 5:19; 8:26).

Jesus chose his apostles to "be with him" before getting into ministry (Mark 3:14), gave them his power and authority to minister for him (Luke 9:1), then told them to teach their followers (presumably including us) all that he had taught them (Matt 28:20), promising that "whoever believes in me will do what I do" (John 14:12). We are to go forth, then, in authority and obedience, imitating Jesus, to enable God's will through the spread of his kingdom, a kingdom spread through acts of power wrapped in acts of love.

Rule 4.6: Both God and Satan are able to provide protection for their followers.

Protection rules seem to have two dimensions to them. First, a certain amount of protection seems to be granted by God or Satan to their followers simply on the basis of their allegiance relationship to that power. Second, though, more protection seems to be available to those who ask and/or claim it in the name of the power. Superseding all claims to protection, however, seems to be the will of the power source. Job and Paul (2 Cor 12:7–9), for example, by God's choice seem to have had protection withdrawn from them. In the case of Gideon, however, God protected the whole nation of Israel until his death, even though he himself had become apostate (Judg 8:28).

Though Satan's power to protect his own is much less than God's and is greatly outmatched when challenged by God in power encounter, demons are usually accomplished at bluffing to protect their turf. Thus, many who are inexperienced in deliverance are tricked in various ways into allowing the demons to stay.

Rule 4.7: Rules for encountering the other kingdom seem to relate to the amount and/or authority of the human support the spirit being has.

When there are large numbers of people and/or people in high position obeying God, the Lord is in a position to order an attack, a power encounter, with the possibility of winning. Under Joshua's leadership, the people of Israel generally, and their leaders in particular, usually listened for and followed God's orders, attacked and won. Earlier in Israel's history, Moses gained great authority with God through his obedience and became usable (in spite of the fact that the people were not necessarily with him at first) by God to attack and win. With Elijah, God pulled off a victory over the prophets of Baal through using the person (Elijah) in the authoritative position of the prophet of Israel (1 Kgs 18).

On the satanic side, as long as the Pharaoh was favorable toward Israel, Satan could not get them. But when a Pharaoh came to power who gave out no favors to Israel because of the prior relationship to Joseph (Exod 1:8), Satan could work with him to attack God's people.

An important part of these rules seems to be the place of obedience to the spirit power. Note, for example, Moses (cited above) and Gideon. In both cases, prior obedience set the stage and continuing obedience resulted in an effective attack. On the other hand, note what happened in the case of Joshua's army attempting to take the city of Ai (Josh 7). Through the disobedience of Achan, a disobedience to God that automatically was an obedience to Satan, the power of God was compromised and the battle to take Ai lost. When Israel obeyed, they took the city (Josh 8:1–29).

Rule 4.8: There are rules for the transmission of spirit power.

Spirit power can be transmitted in a variety of ways. Some of the vehicles most frequently used are words (e.g., prayer, blessing, cursing, dedication, healing), touch (e.g., laying on of hands, 2 Tim 1:6), being in sacred places (e.g., temples, churches, shrines), possession of empowered objects (e.g., objects that have been dedicated, blessed or cursed) and the like. God uses words to transmit his power to humans and empowers us to do the same in a variety of ways. When we bless someone, spiritual power is transmitted through us to that person. In addition, dedicated people, buildings or objects carry the power of the spirit being in whose name they were dedicated.

It is important that the person who attempts to transmit the power of God or Satan have the authority of that being to do it. Note the problem the sons of Sceva ran into when the demons called them on the fact that they were using the name of Jesus without his authority to do so (Acts 19:13–16). On the other hand, even the possessions of Paul who had Jesus' authority were effective in transmitting God's power (Acts 19:12).

Rule 4.9: There are rules for hindering the opposite power as he tries to carry out his will.

Perhaps the most important of these rules is that when people disobey the power to whom they have committed themselves or neglect their relationship with him, they hinder that power from doing what he wants to do. Thus, a primary tactic of Satan is to get God's people to disobey or neglect God. This he does most effectively through either keeping people ignorant of what God desires (2 Cor 4:4) or by deceiving them into disobeying (Gen 3:1–7).

On the enemy's side, I have met many frustrated demons whose major problem was that they could not get the persons in whom they lived to do their will because these persons were busy obeying God. Though the obedience to God practiced by these persons did not succeed in getting rid of the demons, it did weaken them seriously and, thus, hindered them greatly in their attempts to do what they wanted to do. Though through bluff, Satan's angels are often able to succeed very well in their attempts to hinder God's work, they are often frustrated because Christians use the greater power of God to hinder them.

Rule 4.10: There are also rules for breaking the power of God or Satan over one who has pledged allegiance to that power.

Breaking God's or Satan's power over oneself is easily done. The person who has given the rights has the authority to renounce those rights. In either kingdom, those who have been dedicated by others or have committed themselves to the spirit power can simply renounce that commitment and pledge allegiance consciously or unconsciously and in that way they move from one allegiance to the other.

Though coming to Christ is easy, involving a simple pledge of allegiance, the price paid by God to free people from the power of Satan is very high. The rule apparently requires the blood sacrifice of a person who has never sinned by obeying the enemy. In obedience to this rule for breaking empowerment, Jesus came as the Second Adam, met the requirements and sacrificed himself to win our freedom. Faith-allegiance to Jesus plus repentance, then, enable us to take advantage of Jesus' sacrifice to break the power of Satan wielded through our sinfulness. That infinite power, then, also becomes available to us to break the power of Satan wielded through demonic oppression and indwelling.

That oppression and indwelling keeps many non-Christians and not a few Christians in constant captivity. Though allegiance to God redeems Christians, reuniting our human spirits with God's Spirit, Satan can still interfere in the Christian's life under certain circumstances. When we sin, we give him permission to harm our fellowship with God until we repent. If we wallow in sin, we open ourselves up to demonization.

When demons live inside, getting rid of what I call "the garbage" is crucial. This includes such things as commitments, inherited infestation, dedications, curses, wallowing in sinful attitudes and the like. Beyond this, the demons usually have to be cast out through the use of God's power and the will of the person.

The enemy's power over places and things can be broken by the people of God asserting God's authority over them. To break enemy power in artifacts is usually simply a matter of asserting God's power over the item. To break the power over places where it has been entrenched for some time, however, usually requires an expert approach.

Principle 5: Cultural Forms Can Be Empowered

Implicit and sometimes explicit in what has been said above is the fact that, in addition to the empowerment of humans, we have to deal with the empowerment of cultural forms such as words, material objects, places and buildings. The empowerment of words seems to be basic to this whole section since in the empowerment of cultural forms other than words, the words uttered serve as the vehicles through which the other items are empowered.

Rule 5.1: Objects can be dedicated to spirit beings either as they are being made or at a later time.

In many societies it is customary for those who make implements used for worship, work, decoration or other functions to dedicate them to their gods or spirits. In the South Pacific, for example, at least in the past and probably to this day, many peoples routinely dedicated their canoes to their gods. Many groups of Christians dedicate implements used in worship, including sanctuary furnishings, anointing oil, the communion elements and "holy" water. Once dedicated, such objects carry the power of God as did the ark of the covenant and other sacred objects in Old Testament times.

As with the ark (1 Sam 5) and cursed items retained by the Israelites in Joshua's day (Josh 7), however, empowered items in the hands of the other side can cause great disruption. Often it has been found that when missionaries or Christian travelers bring home objects from other societies and keep them in their homes, there is disruption by demons until the objects are either cleansed or gotten rid of. My colleague C. Peter Wagner had such disruption in his home several years ago until he got rid of a group of infested items he and his wife had brought back with them from Bolivia. Unknown to them, these items had been dedicated to evil spirits in Bolivia.

In ministry, we find blessed oil to often (not always) be effective in lessening the power of demons. Blessed water and salt can also be effective as can a blessed cross or Bible. In each case, the power is not in the object itself but in the power of God invested in the item through blessing. In the New Testament, objects such as Paul's handkerchiefs and aprons conveyed God's power for healing and deliverance (Acts 19:12). Some contemporary healers also use such items. I know some who have found baptizing demonized persons in blessed water to be quite effective in deliverance. I have also seen healing happen when people have partaken of blessed Communion elements.

Rule 5.2: Words used on the authority of and in the service of whatever spirit a person serves are empowered by that spirit.

Blessings uttered by his people are empowered by God. So are curses. "Blessings" and curses are likewise empowered by the enemy when his people utter them. Words used to dedicate and for other purposes (e.g., sermonizing, witnessing) are also empowered by the spirit being on whose behalf they are uttered. Among other things, this means we have to be careful how we use our words. Through negative empowered words, for example, I find that many people have cursed themselves and/or those close to them.

We can bless things and persons for specific purposes such as those mentioned under rule 5.1 above. Often when I have blessed people with peace, they have felt the peace come over them. We can bless such things as cars, homes, offices and other things with protection from enemy interference. A woman once told me of a scheme she developed to get her husband saved. Knowing the power of blessing, she blessed his toothbrush with the power of God to open him up to the gospel. Within three weeks he had turned to Christ!

Blessings and curses are under the power of the one who utters them. In Luke 9 and 10, Jesus sent his disciples out to witness, commanding them to bless a home first, then to retract the blessing if they were not welcomed there. The fact that the disciples had put the blessings on meant that they could take them off. Those who have cursed themselves, therefore, can retract/renounce such curses and be free from them. One with superior power can also break the curses/blessings of one with lesser power. Thus, for Christians to break curses put on under satanic power is usually fairly easy once the curse is discovered.

Rule 5.3: Other nonmaterial cultural forms can also be empowered.

Music is frequently empowered through dedication to either God or Satan. So are rituals, dances and other worship activities. The blessing we feel in worship is likely due to a combination of the pleasantness we feel at the human level and the empowerment of God that comes through "anointed" music at the spiritual level.

There are musical groups active in America who openly dedicate their music to Satan and probably some who do so unconsciously. Such music conveys satanic power to its devotees. Christian worship music may be consciously or unconsciously blessed and is, therefore, effective in conveying God's power to those who use it. Blessed music played in our homes and cars is also effective in suppressing any rights the enemy may have to those places. I believe it also serves to protect against satanic attacks.

Rule 5.4: Buildings can likewise be invested with spiritual power.

Church buildings, homes, shrines and other places by means of such dedication can become spiritually "clean." On the other side, buildings can be dedicated to Satan. Or, through regular use for evil purposes (e.g., prostitution, gambling, pornography, homosexual activity, financial swindling, abortions, occult meetings) they can be empowered with satanic power. Masonic lodges, pagan shrines, temples, occult bookstores, some health foods, environmental and martial arts establishments, abortion clinics, offices of occult and sin-enhancing organizations and other buildings dedicated and used for satanic purposes are so invested and are dangerous for Christians to enter without claiming God's protection.

I was once consulted by a mission leader concerning one of his colleagues who seemed to be disruptive during mission meetings. I asked this leader if he spiritually cleansed the office in which they met before each meeting. He did not but started to after our conversation. The disruptive person's behavior changed dramatically. Several teachers have told me they have found their students' behavior changed since they started blessing their classrooms.

Principle 6: Territories and Organizations Can Be Subject to Spirit Power

It appears that the spirit beings that serve God and Satan can be divided roughly into "ground-level" and "cosmic-level" spirits. The latter seem to be more powerful and to deal with groupings of people rather than individuals. We often refer to them as "territorial spirits." Note, however, that their concern is for people more than for territory. Though perhaps land in and of itself is of some interest to them, it is the people within a territory that are their primary focus.

Rule 6.1: Higher- (cosmos-) level spirits on both sides seem to exert what might be referred to as a "force field" influence over territories, buildings and organizations, including nations.

In Daniel 10 reference is made to high-level satanic princes who ruled over Persia and Greece. On God's side, each of the churches of Revelation 1–3 seems to have an angel in charge. Sinful businesses such as prostitution, gambling, abortion, pornography, homosexuality, occult bookstores and the like are often clustered in certain sections of cities, suggesting that there might be ruling spirits in charge of those areas. Those involved in spying out the enemy's activities by mapping geographical areas to detect such activity speak of discernable patterns of this kind. Churches and other Christian organizations and their properties are likely superintended by God's angelic messengers in the same way.

Such "force field" influence extends also to individuals. For, as pointed out in 2 Cor 4:4, our enemy is able to keep the minds of unbelievers in the dark, blinding them to the truth. Indeed, the verse goes on to indicate that Satan is able to counter the force field activity of God, saying that "[Satan] keeps them from seeing the light shining on them, the light that comes from the good news about the glory of Christ, who is the exact likeness of God."

It is this blinding activity of the enemy that Ed Silvoso and others are now learning to nullify through cosmic-level spiritual warfare, leading to impressive conversion and church growth statistics.

Rule 6.2: In order for spirit beings to have authority over territories and organizations, they must have legal rights.

Such rights are given them through the allegiances, dedications and behavior of the humans who now use and have used the territories and organizations in the past. Territories and organizations can be consciously dedicated to the spirit beings to whom those in authority over them are committed. They also seem to be dedicated by the way they are used. On the evil side, evil usage results in dedication to Satan. I'm not sure whether righteous usage can completely break a prior dedication to the enemy. Such dedications, then, continue from generation to generation until broken by the current authority figures.

In Papua New Guinea, I learned that a whole mission compound has been built on territory formerly used for tribal warfare. In an American community I was told that a church and a high school are built on an ancient Indian burial ground. Until the power given the enemy over those territories by the evil activity is broken by the power of God, Satan will continue to have great ability to interfere with God's activities in those places.

Rule 6.3: The rules for breaking spirit power over territories are parallel to those for breaking spirit power over individuals.

What I mean by this rule is that as with individuals we need to look for and cleanse from the "garbage," so with territories. The garbage in individuals as listed in rule 4.10 above includes such things as commitments, inherited infestation, dedications, curses, wallowing in sinful attitudes and the like. For territories, it is crucial to find and break the power of commitments, dedications, curses, sins that have been committed on the land, used for sinful purposes and the like. Agreements made consciously or unconsciously in the past by those in authority over the land that gave the enemy rights must be dealt with. These past rights constitute a major spiritual power thing that has to be encountered and broken.

Examples of such territory would be cities dedicated by Freemasons (e.g., Washington, DC, and several Argentine cities), places where blood has been shed unjustly (e.g., through warfare, through throwing ailing slaves overboard as in the Bermuda Triangle; see McAll, *Healing the Family Tree*) and sections of cities given to violence, prostitution, homosexuality and the like. Just as with individuals, gaining cleansing from sin is an important step in breaking the enemy's power and is crucial to freedom. Areas infected by sinful usage can be cleansed through repentance on the part of those now in authority over them. We call this "identi-ficational repentance." It consists of contemporary representatives of groups who sinned against other groups taking responsibility for the sins of their ancestors and repenting (preferably in pub-lic) to contemporary representatives of the groups wronged. Such ground-level human activity prepares the way for the attack activ-ity spoken of in rule 6.6.

The way the rules work over territories on Satan's side are again parallel to those for individuals. Just as Satan has gained rights over an individual through sin, cursing, dedication and the like, so he has gained rights over territories. The key to breaking those rights is, then, the discovery and dealing with those historical factors.

Rule 6.4: Cosmic-level spirits seem to wield their authority over territories as defined by humans.

The fact that the guardian angel over Persia (Dan 10:13, 21) and the one over Greece (Dan 10:21) are labeled by human territorial names would point in that direction. So would the impression gained by those who study and deal with territorial spirits—that impression being that there are national spirits, regional spirits, spirits over cities, spirits over sections of cities and the like.

A missionary distributing tracts in a small border town along a street that divided Brazil from Uruguay found that people accept-ed the tracts on the Brazil side but refused them on the Uruguay side. Furthermore, some who had refused them on the Uruguay side, received them gladly after they had crossed over to the Bra-zilian side. The missionary's interpretation was that the prayer of Christians on the Brazil side was what made the difference. There was a difference in the enemy's ability to control the response of the people on either side of the human political border between these two countries (see Wagner, *Engaging the Enemy*, 47–48).

Rule 6.5: There seem to be cosmic-level spirits that are in charge of organizations, institutions and activities.

Though some of this has been said above with respect to territory (rule 6.1), we may point here to the probability that there are cosmic-level spirits whose job is to promote pornography, abortion, homosexuality, prostitution, occult organizations and the like. On God's side, then, we know of angels that are assigned to children (Matt 18:10) and to churches (Rev 1–3). Why not to Christian activities such as missionary and other parachurch organizations?

Institutions such as churches, seminaries, Bible schools and the like probably all have high-level spirits assigned to them. So do social institutions such as marriages, governments, educational institutions and the like.

Rule 6.6: There are rules that can be followed to gain protection from or to launch attacks upon spirits assigned to territories and organizations.

Rules such as those given above concerning the importance of praise and worship plus those concerning claiming protection apply here under the protection category. Rules given for breaking spirit power over territories are also applicable.

To attack evil spiritual beings in power encounters, the rules include engaging in prayer (especially intercession and authority praying), repentance, worship, fasting and the like by groups of people committed to God, to each other and to battling the enemy through the use of such weapons. The attackers need to have rid themselves of as much internal "garbage" as possible so that the enemy can find nothing in them to get a grip on (John 14:30).

They then need to give attention to breaking all historical and/or contemporary commitments, curses and dedications holding the territory or organization in Satan's grip along with repentance of any sins committed in that territory (see 6.3 above). Next, in authoritative praying, they may speak to "the spiritual powers in space" (Eph 2:2), laying claim to the territory or organization.

This is what Steve Nicholson, a Vineyard pastor in Evanston, Illinois, did in claiming a certain territory for his church. Over a period of time, in prayer, he proclaimed to the listening satanic spirits that he was taking a specified territory for God. After some time a powerful spirit appeared to him refusing to give him as much territory as he was claiming. At this, he again asserted his claim and succeeded in breaking the power of that spirit (a spirit of witchcraft) and saw his church double in size soon thereafter.

On the satanic side, groups of people in given territories who immerse themselves in sinful activities gain a certain amount of protection against the forces of God. Their activities, furthermore, constitute attacks on God's program, though they merely hold for Satan territory that he already has laid claim to, for now.

Conclusion

There is much that we don't know in the dynamics of power encounter that I have tried to examine above. In attempting to discover the principles and rules that govern the spiritual realm, we are probably about at the level where Western scientists were in their attempts to figure out physical laws a thousand years ago. Nevertheless, it is worth making what we think we understand as explicit as possible, if for no other reason than that others can react to it and advance our understandings by making additions and corrections.

CHAPTER 6

Spiritual Power Inventory

The Christian witness needs to be aware of quite a number of practices (the "inventory") that people use in interaction with their gods and spirits. Among these are witchcraft, sorcery, magic, divination, cursing, both formal and informal and several others. There are practitioners such as shamans, priests and diviners who specialize in performing rites and rituals often in special places, such as shrines, often at special times. To protect themselves from malevolent use of spiritual techniques, then, people use charms and amulets usually on their bodies. We will deal below with a special type of divination called an "ordeal," used to discover guilt or innocence.

God, Gods & Idols

God is a God of power but not of misuse of that power. God wants his power to be used in loving, controlled ways. Therefore, God comes down hard on power practices used for anti-God practices.

Our approach to spiritual power must take into account the strong negative tone of God's pronouncements concerning compromise with regard to other gods, idols and the ways in which their power is engaged. As we have seen, then, the Old Testament is an excellent source from which today's peoples can learn what is and is not allowable.

The Bible is clear that the worship of any god but the true God is not permitted. We are to "worship no god but me [Yahweh]" (Exod 20:3). There are, then, to be no idols made or worshipped because "I am the Lord your God and I tolerate no rivals" (Exod 20:5). And among the warnings in the New Testament is the command at the end of 1 John, "My children, keep yourselves safe from false gods!" (1 John 5:21).

Perhaps the clearest indication of what God feels about his people having relationships with other gods is found in the story of the people of Israel at Peor in Numbers 25. God became very angry at the Israelite leaders who attended feasts with Moabite women "where the god of Moab was worshipped" and where "the Israelites ate the food and worshipped the god Baal of Peor" (Num 25:2–3). God was so angry at them that he commanded that those who had participated in that worship should be killed publicly (Num 25:4). Then, when an Israelite man openly challenged the prohibition by taking a Midianite woman into his tent, God commended Phinehas, Aaron's grandson, for killing both the man and the woman, saying, "Because of what Phinehas has done, I am no longer angry with the people of Israel . . . [and] he and his descendants are permanently established as priests, because he did not tolerate any rivals to me and brought about forgiveness for the people's sin" (Num 25:11, 13). Contextualization of idolatry, then, is condemned for God's people.

Several other practices are also forbidden to God's people and labeled as the reasons why God gave his people the right to drive out the inhabitants of Palestine. In Deut 18:9–13 several of these things are listed and labeled "disgusting practices." The practices listed there are: sacrificing children, divination, looking for omens, using spells or charms and consulting spirits of the dead. The text says, "God hates people who do these disgusting things, and that is why he is driving those nations out of the land as you advance" (Deut 18:12).

Some people read in the Old Testament and conclude that God is bloodthirsty and unfair. Such a belief does not recognize the spiritual component of human existence. Therefore, they are ignoring just how much God hates the fact that people are using their free will to turn their backs on God. They give their allegiance to satanic spirits.

It is clear that God forbids many common pagan practices involving spiritual power. God does not tolerate appeasing pagan gods or spirits or seeking information, health, wealth or blessing from them. His answer to the quest for these things is to turn to him and allow him to take care of the opposing spirits and to provide the blessings we need.

It is frightening to think what such total condemnation says to today's "dual allegiance" Christians—those who have committed themselves to Christ but also continue to seek spiritual power from traditional shamans, priests and shrines. Since God tolerates no rivals, the situation is serious if going to these other gods and spirits constitutes worship. I trust, though, that God takes into account both the ignorance and the Christian dedication of such people and their missionaries. Perhaps what the prophet Elisha said to Naaman in 2 Kings 5 offers some hope. After Naaman was healed and committed himself to the God of Israel, he asked the prophet how he should now behave when he is required by his master to accompany him to a pagan temple. Elisha indicates that God will be understanding.

In attempting to see biblical Christianity contextualized, then, we recognize that God allows no rivals. Though he allowed Israel's belief in many gods to continue for some time, he insisted that there be no compromise with regard to allegiance—no rivals. And no contacting spirits of dead people. Places of worship and even rituals and transition rites such as circumcision and baptism, used by pagans in prechristian observances can, however, be captured, purified and used to honor the true God.

Witchcraft & Sorcery

Most of the peoples of the world assume that spiritual power can be directed toward others with the express aim of harming them. We label such concepts "witchcraft" and "sorcery." Though technically sorcery is conscious and deliberate, while witchcraft is considered to be unconscious, the term witchcraft is commonly used to cover both conscious and unconscious malevolent spiritual activity.

Shamans, diviners and other purveyors of spiritual power are regularly sought by people who feel they have been wronged, to conduct rituals, usually involving magic, designed to harm those against whom they wish to take revenge. In addition, the spirits of witches are believed to be able to astral project, leaving their bodies, usually at night, to go to other people and places to cause harm, often to the innocent.

In many societies it is assumed that illness, accident and death are never natural occurrences. Commonly, then, it is assumed that when a person dies, becomes ill or has an accident it is the result of witchcraft or sorcery. It is then the task of a diviner or a "witch doctor" to ascertain who has caused the death and why. Various forms of divination and ordeal are used to identify the culprit. People often wear charms to protect themselves against witchcraft and magic.

The fear of witchcraft is a major factor in most societies and an important concern of many churches and witch-finding organizations. Since witches are supposed to harm people unconsciously, those accused by such groups are often quite unaware of their supposed guilt.

A common form of witchcraft is the evil eye. This is the belief that some people, whether consciously or unconsciously, can direct evil power toward others, especially children, simply by staring at them. Looks plus compliments directed toward children are considered especially dangerous since such notice may incite the attention of evil spirits. Parents will, therefore, make their children less attractive to avoid drawing attention from those believed to have the evil eye or from other malevolent spirits who may be jealous of the child.

Magic is another important part of witchcraft. It depends on words and formulas with the expectation that if they are said just right, the result is expected to be automatic. Magic is thought to be impersonal. What many miss is that it is empowered by invisible spirits. Magic is usually used for negative purposes by someone against someone else and for that reason is feared.

Missionaries who ignore or summarily dismiss witchcraft, magic and sorcery beliefs and practices often drive them underground. The practices and beliefs do not change; they are only removed from public scrutiny. Missionaries must find sensitive ways to understand and deal not only with the beliefs and practices themselves, but with the functions such beliefs and practices serve within the societies in which they are found. The existence of these spirit practices provide countless opportunities for power encounters.

Curses & Blessings

A curse is an utterance in which a person calls on supernatural power to bring harm to the one cursed. Curses are the opposite of blessings, usually making use of satanic power rather than, as with blessings, employing the power of God. Though words are usually used, the power is not in the words but flows from the supernatural being who empowers the words.

The Bible takes curses and cursing seriously, assuming that people have the authority to invoke supernatural power in this way. The words are used about two hundred times in the Scriptures. The term "anathema" (1 Cor 16:22), often seen as a powerful curse in Scripture, is instead a formula of excommunication with which a person is turned over to God for punishment (see Brown, "Curse").

The authority Christians have to curse is neither to be taken lightly (Jas 3:8–10) nor to be abused. Indeed, both Jesus (Luke 6:28) and Paul (Rom 12:14) admonish us to bless rather than to curse those who hurt us. The Jews who participated in the crucifixion called down on themselves a very powerful curse when they said, "Let the punishment for his death fall on us and our children!" (Matt 27:25).

Cursing seems to be very much alive today. Missionaries from various parts of the world report situations in which parcels of land, buildings, artifacts and missionaries themselves and/or their family members have had directed at them negative words that were followed by strange occurrences. Several instances have been reported of illness or other misfortune affecting everyone who lived in mission homes built on land the people consider cursed. In many cases, the situation has been alleviated through claiming the authority of Christ to break the apparent curses. In addition, those involved in praying with people for inner healing report great change when certain negative emotional and spiritual symptoms are dealt with by claiming the authority of Christ to break curses (see Kraft, *Defeating Dark Angels*).

Divination

Divination is the practice of seeking secret knowledge, usually of the future, by occult means. A wide variety of techniques are used with the expectation that insight will be provided by supernatural beings or power. Divination is and has ever been a very widespread practice among non-Christian peoples and, unfortunately, among many who call themselves Christians.

Diviners are specialists in using the techniques of divination to discover the information sought by their clients. The power to gain such information is assumed to be obtained either by directly petitioning a spirit or magically, through the correct performance of given rituals. Most of those who specialize in working with satanic power combine divination with their other activities. Shamans, spirit mediums, priests of various cults, witches, sorcerers, witch doctors and the like usually practice divination in addition to whatever else they do.

Among the techniques used are dreams, horoscopes and astrological tables, water witching, examination of entrails or tea leaves, observing the activities of birds or other animals, the positions of coals or stones, cards, dice, crystals and palmistry. In Scripture we find reference to divination through examining a dead animal's liver (Ezek 21:21), throwing down arrows (Ezek 21:21), using a cup of water (Gen 44:5), casting lots (John 1:7), astrology (Isa 47:13), consulting the dead (technically known as necromancy, Lev 19:31; Is 8:19). God's disapproval of the use of such techniques to gain information from evil spirits (Lev 20:6) is to be carefully distinguished from his willingness to use such a technique as casting lots under his guidance to discern his will (Josh 18:6, 8, 10; Acts 1:26).

As mentioned, divination is very common today. The techniques used are empowered by demons with very real results. Diviners are able to use Satan's communication system to find things that have been lost, make predictions concerning the future that, if believed, bear startling fruit and to thoroughly impress those who know no greater power.

Those who would present Christianity in a way that is attractive to the majority of the peoples of the world need to take such manifestations of satanic power seriously and confront it in power encounters. Jesus came into a power-oriented world (like ours) and both showed us how to use God's power and passed on his authority and power to us (Luke 9:1; John 14:12) to enable us to confront and defeat the enemy in contexts where he is influencing people through divination.

Ordeal

A specialized form of divination is called "ordeal." Trial by ordeal is used in many societies to discover secret information regarding the guilt or innocence of a person accused of a crime. Ordeals may involve such things as forcing accused persons to dip their hand in hot oil, swallow poison, have a hot knife pressed against their bodies or some other act with the understanding that if they are harmed they are guilty. In Num 5:11–31, Moses is commanded to instruct the Israelites to use an ordeal involving an oath and the drinking of "bitter water" to discern the guilt or innocence of a wife suspected of adultery.

Dedication

One category of cosmic-level spirits is assigned to trees, bodies of water, tools, household or other objects through dedication of these objects to a given god or spirit. Such spirits are also assigned to rituals, certain music and other nonmaterial entities through dedication. Taiwanese speak of gods attached to stoves, furniture, clothing and other household goods. In many societies, all tools, farming implements and other items associated with the maintaining of life and well-being are routinely dedicated to their gods or spirits, as are all items used in religious rituals. When such items are obtained by travelers and taken home as souvenirs, the spirits in them can cause disruption in their homes.

It is well known that certain musical groups in Western countries are openly committed to Satan and their music dedicated to him. Video games such as Dungeons and Dragons and, probably, certain movies are also dedicated to Satan. The dedication of artistic productions, often to be used for religious purposes, has been the custom of many of the world's peoples for centuries. People regularly become demonized through contact with such nonmaterial demonically infested entities.

It is important that we recognize Satan's ability to heal and bless those who come to places dedicated to him, such as shrines. For too long Christians have tried to ignore Satan's counterfeiting and the attraction it has for many, both non-Christian and Christian, who seek enough spiritual power to enable them to live their lives reasonably well.

Spirits attached to such material or nonmaterial entities are usually not difficult to deal with in the power of Christ. Once there is a suspicion that a given item is infested, all we usually have to do is to claim the power of Christ to cancel all enemy rights. If a material item has a specifically religious purpose, however, it may be judicious to destroy it after breaking its power. Nonmaterial entities may raise other problems, since the lyrics of songs may be immoral as well as dedicated to Satan. And, with both material and nonmaterial entities, the biggest battle may be against the former meanings even if the cultural forms are spiritually purified. With most items it is possible to first cancel all enemy power and then to bless them with the power of Jesus to complete their transformation from enemies to friends. Only after the empowerment has been thus broken is it wise to begin to deal with the meaning problems.

With regard to shrines, a more creative approach may be worth experimenting with. In Japan, for example, it is clear that those who come to the Shinto shrines are seeking the same kinds of blessings that Jesus offers to Christians. Might we not propose, then, that churches capture this custom by sponsoring Christian shrines where people could receive prayer in Jesus' name for such requests? For Japanese people are used to going to shrines whenever they feel the need for power, rather than at set times such as Sunday morning. So, even if such shrine concerns as blessings for marriage and for school examinations, healing of various ailments and relationships, fertility for themselves or loved ones and other such things are prayed for in church (and they often are not), Christian shrines would be more appropriate places to deal with them.

Christian shrines would, of course, differ in several respects from Shinto shrines. For example, they would involve people who would pray for those who come, not simply a statue to pour water over. And those with further interest would be encouraged to attend regular meetings (Sundays and other days) sponsored by the church. There would be literature there as well and the shrines would be advertised, as other shrines are, on the trains and busses. And those who pray for people could be young people with various spiritual gifts, thus enabling youth to minister in ways acceptable to Japanese even before they are old enough to be socially accepted in leadership positions.

Since the rules for spiritual activity are the same for Satan and for God, a parallel situation exists when we bless or dedicate objects in the name of Jesus. Anointing oil, for example, is empowered to convey God's power when we bless or dedicate it. So it is also when we bless or dedicate buildings, such as church buildings or our homes and work space such as a teacher's classroom or an office. Any substance or space, including homes, churches, work implements, vehicles, musical instruments, food, holy water, even salt can be so dedicated. So can rituals such as baptism, worship music, baby or building dedications and the like. When so dedicated to God, such items, places or nonmaterial entities become conveyers of God's blessing in the same way that satanic dedication enables such entities to convey his power.

Whether God invests such items and places with angels as Satan invests things and places dedicated to him with demons, I don't know. I suspect that he does, however, since it is God's methods that Satan is counterfeiting. It may, then, be appropriate to think of angels inhabiting things and places dedicated to God as well as demonic infestation of things and places dedicated to Satan.

An important part of spiritual warfare, then, is the retaking from Satan of things, places and nonmaterial entities that God created to serve his purposes, just as we retake persons from the enemy when we free them from demons. Though some (e.g., Hunt and McMahon, *Seductcion of Christianity*) counsel Christians to retreat from the enemy by destroying or refusing to use items and practices employed by Satan in such occultic involvements as New Age, I believe the Christian posture should be with most things to break the satanic power, then to take things back from the enemy, whether at ground or at cosmic level.

Ancestors

Given the concern of family members for those who have died, what a stroke of genius on the part of Satan to convince people that their loved ones are still alive (true) and that they continue to actively participate in human life (false)! By so doing, demons are able to work freely, disguised as ancestors. And since they already know everything about that ancestor, they can do an excellent job of impersonation and, in the process, exert a great amount of control over the people. Demons, posing as ancestors, with power to give and to take away, can bind people to false beliefs and the rituals that go with them in a most impressive way.

Given the appropriateness of such contextualization from Satan's point of view, the question to be raised is what we can do about it. Most of the peoples of the world have long since bought the lie that it is really their loved ones who are receiving and responding to their attentions. And it is not easy to get them to understand that what they have been believing for generations is a lie.

Academics, with no experience with the demonic world themselves, argue about whether it is really the ancestors who appear to their living family members. Some point to the passage concerning King Saul's excursion to the "witch of Endor" (1 Sam 28:3–19). But this account and the fact that at the transfiguration Moses and Elijah appeared to Jesus (Luke 9:28–31), are best interpreted as specific times when God allowed deceased people to return for specific purposes. They have nothing to do with the possibility that ancestors are conscious of and interacting with human life. More to the point is the statement in Heb 12:1 that "we have this large crowd of witnesses round us." But, though this verse may mean that the deceased are able to watch us, it gives no indication that they can participate in human life.

So, we are left scripturally with no encouragement to believe that the dead interact with the living. And, in fact, we are warned sternly not to attempt to contact the dead (Lev 19:31; Deut 18:11). The practice of diviners seeking information about this life, and especially about the future, from the deceased is well known, both in Scripture and in contemporary societies. We learn from Deut 18:12 that "the Lord your God hates people who do these disgusting things."

It is a challenge to faithfully communicate the truth of God's attitude toward such deception to those who have for generations offered sacrifices and done other acts of worship to these supposed ancestors. "Where are my ancestors now," they ask, often adding that they want to be with them for eternity even if they are in hell. With regard to where they are, I believe God's words to Abraham apply when he asked, "Will not the God of all the universe do right?" (Gen 18:25). And Jesus helps us (and them) greatly when he tells the story of the rich man and his servant Lazarus (Luke

16:19–31). For, if any of our ancestors are in hell, according to that story, they desperately want us, the living, to be able to avoid going to be where they are.

To free people spiritually from satanic deception in ancestral matters, we will have to deal with demonization early on. For such commitment to enemy spirits is an invitation for them to live inside. And since this commitment has been going on for generations, with accompanying dedications of each newborn to the spirits, what we are dealing with are ancestral, family spirits inherited from a person's parents. These need to be banished. So do the spirits inhabiting the ancestral tablets and/or other paraphernalia associated with the reverence and/or worship accorded them.

The difficulties involved in considering how to contextualize ancestor beliefs and practices are challenging. Will people agree to speak to Jesus, instead of directly to the dead, asking him to convey any messages he chooses to the ancestors? Will they, then, replace the pictures of ancestors with that of Jesus, or place his in the center and the others in secondary places? And if they do that, are the meanings in their minds changed enough? Are the experiments in Papua New Guinea designed to present Jesus as the Great Ancestor working? And are they theologically valid? We need to hear of more experiments in this area.

Reincarnation

Reincarnation is another area of demonic deception. Since demons know people's lives in detail, it is easy for them to simply tell people someone else's life as if it was their own past life. This is how they fool Westerners into believing something that is new in the West. It's even easier to fool Hindus who have philosophized the recycling of lives. As in many of Satan's activities, he has trained them to perpetuate his deceit themselves, without much, if any, of his help.

The Scripture is clear that "everyone must die once, and after that be judged by God" (Heb 9:27). There is, therefore, no scriptural allowance for anyone to be reborn into another earthly existence. God has created each of us unique and eternal. This belief, therefore, like idolatry and divination, cannot be contextualized. Dealing with the demons of reincarnation in power encounter may, however, be the first step toward freeing people from this lie.

Shrines and Dedicated Places

It is important that we recognize Satan's ability to heal and bless those who come to places dedicated to him. For too long Western Christians have tried to ignore Satan's counterfeiting and the attraction it has for many who seek enough spiritual power to enable them to live their lives reasonably well. These places and the power they convey must be taken seriously, however.

But they can be captured, satanic power broken and dedicated to the true God, as were high places, altars and rituals in the Old Testament. Or, Christian power centers could be constructed after patterns familiar to recently converted people. In Japan, for example, where it is the custom for people to go to power places whenever they feel the need, Christian shrines could be constructed that look like Shinto shrines but function under the authority and power of Jesus Christ. Such shrines would look to Japanese like places where their power needs can be met. They would not look like foreign incursions into Japanese life where knowledge about Christianity is dispensed but the power people seek in religious activity is missing.

Such shrines would, of course, differ in several respects from normal Shinto shrines. For one thing, the land on which they stand would be spiritually cleansed of satanic power and dedicated to God. In addition, such shrines would involve people who would pray for those who come, not simply (as in Japan) a statue to pour water over. And it would be recommended at these shrines that those with further interest attend regular meetings (Sundays and other days) sponsored by the church. There would be literature there as well and the shrines would be advertised, as other shrines are, on the trains. And those who pray for people could be girls and young boys, thus providing for the youth a kind of ministry for which they would usually have to wait several years.

Condemn or Contextualize?

We have surveyed some of the aspects of spiritual power that need to be carefully but effectively dealt with in any consideration of appropriate Christianity. It is unfortunate that in most situations missionized from the West these issues have not been taken seriously or, if the presence of satanic power is recognized, the whole culture is often condemned. People have, therefore, moved into an allegiance to Christ without fully giving up their previous allegiances to traditional spirits and gods. This and many other problems that have arisen because of the lack of attention to the contextualization of spiritual power. Christian witnesses desperately need to face and work through to discover answers that are both scripturally and culturally appropriate.

The basic question to ask is, should this custom be contextualized or condemned? I asked this question of some Japanese Christians concerning Japanese shrines to stimulate thinking in this area. They weren't all in agreement. But as they saw the possibility of canceling satanic power while keeping as many cultural forms as possible and using disempowered customs, the contextualization option made more sense.

God loves culture. So does Satan. Both use many of the same activities. For God's activities to win, they need to be cleansed from satanic power. We call the confronting of these forms of satanic interference in the human arena "spiritual warfare."

CHAPTER 7

Applying the Insights

SPIRITUAL WARFARE IS A topic that is both biblical and contemporary. As the Apostle Paul has said, "We are not fighting [merely] against human beings but against the wicked spiritual forces in the heavenly world, the rulers, authorities, and cosmic powers of this dark age" (Eph 6:12). And those of us who approach counseling and broader ministry from a spiritual and Spirit-led perspective soon discover that Satan is alive and active today on both "ground" and cosmic levels.

Whether it is the temptation in the garden of Eden (Gen 3), the constant conflict between Yahweh and the various gods of Israel's neighbors (e.g., Baal, Ashteroth, Chemosh, etc.) over the allegiance of Israel (e.g., Josh 24:14–24), the discussion between God and Satan over Job (Job 1), the hindrance by the "Prince of Persia" of the answer to Daniel's prayer (Dan 10:13), the temptations of Jesus by Satan (Luke 4:1–13) or the various references in Acts (e.g., 16:16–18; 19:11–20), the Epistles (e.g., 1 Cor 10:18–21; 2 Cor 10:4–5; 1 Pet 5:8; 1 John 3:8) and Revelation (e.g., chs 2–3), it is clear that Scripture portrays human life as lived in a context of continual warfare between the kingdom of God and the kingdom of Satan. And this conflict centers around power encounters.

Though the concept has been questioned by ivory tower theoreticians, spiritual warfare is an important biblical reality and, for those of us who are practitioners, a continual existential reality.

Jesus treated Satan and demonic forces as real foes, frequently casting out demons and thus setting free people he called "captives" and "oppressed" (Luke 4:18). Such language is warfare language. Furthermore, he calls Satan "the ruler of this world" (John 14:30) but, according to John, Jesus' work will result in the destruction of Satan's works (e.g., 1 John 3:8) and, according to the author of Hebrews, of Satan himself (Heb 2:14). In a similar vein, Paul refers to Satan as "the evil god of this world" who "keeps [people] from seeing the light shining on them" because "their minds have been kept in the dark" (2 Cor 4:4), and John says "the whole world is under the rule of the Evil One" (1 John 5:19). These, too, are images that point to the need for warfare on the part of God's forces to defeat the enemy.

Like most of the world today, biblical peoples saw the world as populated by enemy spirits that could cause trouble if they were not properly dealt with. Unfortunately, through most of its history, the people of Israel chose to deal with these spirits as the animistic peoples around them did, rather than as God commanded them to. So God is constantly warning his people against worshiping the gods of the nations around them and punishing them when they disobey (e.g., Exod 34:11–17). We know that our God is a patient God. He has demonstrated this countless times in his dealings with human beings. But there are areas of life, especially those dealing with the counterfeiting of his power-oriented activities in which he has made it clear that there is to be no compromise.

Note, as one of many examples, what God said to Solomon in 1 Kings 11 (esp. vv. 9–13) concerning the penalty he would have to pay for disobeying him by turning to other gods. God was angry with Solomon and took the kingdom away from his son because of Solomon's idolatry. In Acts 5, then, Peter asks Ananias why he "let Satan take control" of him (v. 3) that he should lie to the Holy Spirit about the price of the property he had sold. And in 1 Cor 10:20–21 we are warned against eating what has been offered to demons. This warning, then, is given even more sternly in Rev 2:14 and 20.

But Jesus came "to destroy what the devil had done" (1 John 3:8) and gives his followers "power and authority to drive out all demons and to cure diseases" (Luke 9:1, 2) and to do the works that he himself had done while on earth (John 14:12). We can't be either biblical or relevant without a solid approach to spiritual power and encounter that involves us in a war between God and Satan. Unfortunately, pastors, missionaries and others who seek to minister in the name of Jesus Christ have usually been blinded by a Western worldview that ignores this facet of biblical teaching and social concern. However, if we are to be truly biblical and effective in following our master, we need to learn biblically legitimate and culturally appropriate approaches to such areas of Christian experience as warfare prayer, deliverance from demons, healing, blessing and cursing, territorial spirits, and dedications.

Prayer and Obedience in Spiritual Warfare

Certain principles govern the way spiritual power operates in the universe (see Kraft, *Behind Enemy Lines*). Among them is the scriptural fact that there is a very close relationship between what goes on in human life and what goes on in the spirit realm. This fact leads to better understandings of the ways in which prayer and obedience affect what goes on in the heavenlies.

When the veil is thrown back on interactions between God and Satan, we note that, at least on some occasions, Satan seeks, and sometimes obtains, special permission from God to disrupt human lives (e.g., Job 1; Luke 22:31–32). We learn, then, from Dan 10:13 (an answer to prayer delayed by a demonic being) and 2 Cor 4:4 (blinding unbelievers) that the enemy can sometimes be successful in thwarting God's plans. See also 2 Pet 3:9 where we are told that God "does not want anyone to be destroyed," but Scripture indicates that many will be lost, because we allow the devil's influence in human affairs. In addition, we see throughout Scripture, examples of people greatly enabling Satan to do his work through their obedience to Satan and disobedience to God. Satan thus wins many battles in spiritual warfare.

The other side of the warfare motif in Scripture shows, however, that humans can do things that thwart the enemy's plans, such as prayer and other acts of obedience to God. Since the relationship between the spirit and human worlds is very close, it becomes clear that whatever is done in the human world has great influence in the spirit world. One of the rules seems to be that when humans honor and obey a spirit being, that being is enabled to do more of what he wants to in the human arena. Thus, when people obey God, God is able to do more of his will among humans than otherwise would be possible. When, then, people obey Satan, Satan is enabled to do more of his will.

Prayer, then, along with fasting, repentance, forgiveness, righteousness and every other attitude and behavior that humans do in obedience to God, can be seen as power encounters, acts of war and means of enabling God to accomplish his plans in the human realm. When we pray as Jesus taught us to pray, "Our Father in heaven; May your holy name be honored" and "may your Kingdom come; may your will be done on earth as it is in heaven" and "forgive us the wrongs we have done, as we forgive the wrongs that others have done to us" and "do not bring us to hard testing, but keep us safe from the Evil One" (Matt 6:9–13), we are partnering with God to enable him to defeat the enemy and to do his will in our lives.

The term "prayer" is, however, used to label several different kinds of obedience to God. When we pray, we ask for things as Jesus commanded us to do (John 15:7; 16:24), we confess our sins (1 John 1:9), we thank God (Eph 5:20) and we intercede for others as Jesus did in John 17:1–26. There are, however, two other types of activity usually referred to as prayer that, along with intercession, are especially related to spiritual warfare. These are what I call "intimacy prayer" and "authority prayer" (Kraft, *I Give You Authority*, 49–52).

Intimacy prayer is what Jesus practiced when he went off to deserted places to spend time alone with the Father (e.g., Matt 14:23; Luke 6:12; 9:28). This type of prayer is basically being with God in fellowship, conversation and listening to him for direction.

It is, then, what Jesus said is necessary between him and us if we are to bear the fruit he expects us to bear (John 15:1–17).

Authority prayer should not, I believe, be called prayer, though we regularly speak of praying for healing or deliverance. It is, rather, the taking of Jesus' authority over conditions that are against God's will and asserting his power against that of the enemy. When we follow Jesus' example, encountering demons and commanding them to release their grip and to leave a person, we are asserting the authority Jesus gave us (Luke 9:1) to do his will in freeing that person from Satan. Likewise when we assert his authority in healing people, blessing people or objects, breaking the enemy's power over objects or places and the like. Most of what is discussed below assumes that this kind of "praying" will be used to wage the warfare we are called to wage against our enemy.

Animism vs. God-Given Authority

Most of the world, including most of the adherents of "world religions," practice what anthropologists and missiologists call "animism." This is the belief, and the practices that go with that belief, that the world is full of spirits that can hurt us unless we are careful to appease them. Animists may or may not believe in a high god. When they do, he is usually seen as benign and thus in little, if any, need of attention. All animists agree, however, that the dangerous spirits need to be watched and kept happy. In addition, most animists believe that evil spirits can inhabit material objects and places such as certain mountains (e.g., OT high places), trees, statues (e.g., idols), rocks (e.g., the Ka'aba in Mecca), rivers (e.g., the Ganges in India), territories, fetishes, charms and any other thing or place that is dedicated to the spirits. Animists also believe in magic and the ability of at least certain people to convey power via curses, blessings, spells and the like.

Many Westerners, unacquainted with animism, have difficulty with the fact that the Bible both recognizes the validity of the power and the power techniques practiced by animists and teaches us to use similar techniques based on similar principles.

The deceptive thing is that much of what God does and endorses looks on the surface like what animists do. There is a reason, but those without experience and understanding of what's going on in the interaction between the spirit world and the human world can easily miss it.

The reason why animism and Christianity look so similar is that the basic difference between them and us is not the presence or absence of power but the source of that power. In areas such as healing, dedicating and blessing, for example, we and they have the capability of doing essentially the same things but the source of their power is Satan, the source of ours is God. We learn both from Scripture and from practical experience that many, if not all of the rules that apply to God's interactions with humans also apply to the ways the enemy interacts with us. For example, obedience to God in prayer, worship, sacrifice and service enables him to carry out his purposes in the world. On the other side, obedience to Satan in these same ways enables him to accomplish his purposes. The importance of obedience and the fact that this is a warfare issue are thus underlined.

For example, animists believe that objects such as idols or implements used in religious rituals may be dedicated to gods or spirits and thus contain spiritual power. Christians believe that objects can be dedicated to our God and thus convey his power (e.g., Paul's handkerchiefs, the ark of the covenant, the communion elements, anointing oil). On the surface, containing and conveying power look the same, especially since what animists believe to be power contained in objects is in reality satanic power conveyed by such objects. For another example, animist diviners, shamans, priests, etc., can heal with the power of Satan. God, of course, also heals. The fact that satanic healing leads sooner or later to captivity and misery is not immediately apparent to the one healed. Nor is the fact that God's healing leads to freedom and peace. On the surface, both types of healing look the same and people whose primary concern is for the healing rather than for a relationship with the healer are easily deceived, especially since demons seem often to work faster than God does.

Our authority as Christians versus the authority Satan can give his followers is an important issue at this point. When we exercise the power and authority Jesus gives us to do things animists do, such as healing, casting out demons, blessing people and objects, dedicating buildings, praying for rain or against floods, we are not animists. For we are working in God's power, not Satan's. We are fighting the battle against Satan, not capitulating to him. We are simply exercising the authority Jesus gave his disciples (Luke 9:1) and told them to teach their followers (Matt 28:19).

We may summarize some of the major issues in this discussion by means of the following chart designed to show many of the contrasts between animism and God-given authority. Note again that the primary expressions of each of these areas will look very similar at the surface level. It is in the underlying power and motivations that they differ. The weapons of our warfare are the same as those employed by the counterfeiter, Satan, but the source of the power by which we use these weapons and the source of our authority to use these weapons is God.

	ANIMISM	GOD-GIVEN AUTHORITY
POWER	Believed to be contained in people & objects	God conveys his power through people & objects
NEED (in order to utilize spiritual power)	Felt need to learn how to manipulate spirit power thru magic or authority over spirits	We are to submit to God & learn to work with him in the exercise of power & authority from him
ONTOLOGY (what is really going on)	Power from Satan: he is the one who manipulates	Power from God: he empowers & uses us

GOD	God is good but distant, therefore ignore him	God is good, therefore relate to him. He is close and involved with us
SPIRITS	Fearful & can hurt us, therefore appease them	They are defeated, therefore assert God's authority over them
PEOPLE	Victims of capricious spirits who never escape from being victims	People are captives, but we can assert Jesus' authority to free them
COST	Those who receive power from Satan suffer great tragedy later	Those who work with God experience love and power throughout life
HOPE	No hope	We win

Satan is very good at protecting himself from what he knows to be a power much greater than his. He knows that God has infinitely more power than he has and that Jesus passed this power on to us, his followers. Satan's primary strategy, therefore, is to keep God's people ignorant and deceived so that we cannot use God's power against him.

Three Crucial Dimensions

In any employment of power encounters in spiritual warfare, we need to keep our focus balanced. For spiritual power in Scripture is never an end in and of itself. The aim of power encounters and of spiritual warfare, is freedom. And this freedom provides the basis from which the Christian can operate in two other crucial dimensions: the allegiance-relationship dimension and the truth-understanding dimension. These two, plus the power-freedom dimension are what I am calling the three crucial dimensions of

Christianity. These dimensions are highlighted by Jesus in Luke 9:11 where after the Twelve had returned from their first teaching and healing excursion and a large crowd had gathered, Jesus "welcomed them, spoke to them about the kingdom of God, and healed those who needed it." Jesus' welcome was a relationship-building act, his speaking to the crowd an impartation of truth to help people understand, and his healing a manifestation of the power of God to bring freedom.

The first and most important of these dimensions is the allegiance-relationship dimension. When Jesus' followers came back from that power-filled excursion into the towns and villages of Galilee, reporting with excitement that "even the demons obeyed us when we gave them a command in your name" (Luke 10:17), Jesus cautioned them and pointed them to something more important. That more important thing is our relationship with the God who provides the power. This relationship, resulting in our names being written in heaven (Luke 10:20) should, according to Jesus, be a greater cause of rejoicing than even our power over demons.

So, as crucial as the power issue is to bring freedom to respond to Christ, the allegiance-relationship issue is even more important even in spiritual warfare and power encounter. As biblical Christians, we've recognized the need to emphasize a commitment to Christ resulting in a freeing and saving relationship with him. When people are encountered with the claims of Christ and respond positively, the most important spiritual battle is won. So, in focusing on the very important encounter and spiritual power dimension, we must be careful not to de-emphasize or neglect all the love and other fruits of the Spirit that flow from the allegiance-relationship dimension.

Nor dare we neglect what I am calling the truth-understanding dimension. Jesus spent most of his time teaching, demonstrating and leading his followers into truth. But, contrary to Western understandings of truth, this is to be an experienced truth, not simply an intellectual truth. For, in keeping with the implications of the Greek and Hebrew words for truth, John 8:32 should read, "you will experience the truth, and the truth will set you free." That continual experiencing of the truth, then, leads to ever deepening understandings both of the truth dimension of Christianity and also of the power-freedom and allegiance-relationship dimensions.

For this truth-understanding dimension is, according to John 8:31, based on obedience to Jesus within the relationship. And all bearing of fruit, including the fruit of spiritual power, is dependent, according to John 15:1–17, on our abiding in a close relationship with Christ.

So, the three crucial dimensions of our Christian experience are our relationship to Christ with all the love and obedience that entails, the understanding that comes from continually experiencing his truth and the freedom Jesus gives us through the exercise of spiritual power that frees us from the enemy's captivity (Luke 4:18–19). This same power, then, is given to us by Jesus to use as he used it in power encounters and spiritual warfare, always as a means of expressing God's love. We are, then, to encounter people and the enemy in appropriate ways with a balance of allegiance, truth and power encounters. Any approach to Christianity and to spiritual warfare that neglects or ignores any of these three dimensions is incomplete and unbalanced.

Levels of Spiritual Warfare

There are at least two levels of spiritual warfare in focus in Scripture. The lower level is what I call "ground-level warfare." The upper level, then, is ordinarily known as "cosmic-level warfare" (called "strategic-level warfare" by Wagner, *Confronting the Powers*, 19–20).

When Jesus and the apostles cast demons out of people, they were engaged in power encounters at ground-level. When, then, Elijah confronted the Baal gods by spiritually attacking their prophets (1 Kgs 18) and Moses confronted the gods of Egypt by staging a series of "power encounters" with Pharaoh and his priests (Exod 7–11), they were engaging in cosmic-level warfare. So were the angel assigned to carry the answer to Daniel's prayer and the "Prince of Persia," though this is another type of cosmic-level conflict.

Note, however, that even cosmic-level warfare has a ground-level dimension. For it is the human representatives of the cosmic gods that engage in the humanly visible part of the battle. Though it is not as obvious, ground-level warfare also has an invisible cosmic dimension. For the ground-level demons are under the authority of cosmic-level spirits and, ultimately, of Satan himself (a cosmic-level being).

Ground-level warfare involves dealing with the spirits that inhabit people (demons). Indwelling spirits or demons may be of at least three kinds: family, occult (e.g., those of non-Christian religions, New Age, Freemasonry) and "ordinary" (e.g., those attached to emotions such as anger and fear, those of lust, death, homosexuality). Family spirits, gaining their power through the dedication of each generation of children to them, are usually the most powerful of the ground-level demons. Occult spirits, gaining their power through invitation, are usually (though not always) stronger than the ordinary demons. The strength of all ground-level demons is calibrated to the amount of spiritual and emotional "garbage" in the person and they are all weakened by dealing with those problems and dispatched in the same way (see Kraft, *Defeating Dark Angels* and *Deep Wounds*).

Note that the fact that demonic strength is a function of the amount and kind of garbage the demon(s) are attached to. This means that demons are a secondary problem. The garbage is the primary problem. Therefore, in seeking to heal a demonized person, we go after the garbage first to take away the demon's power. This will assure that the demon is at his weakest when we begin to deal with him.

Cosmic-level warfare involves dealing with at least five kinds of higher-level spirits: (1) territorial spirits over cities, regions and nations such as those mentioned in Dan 10:13 and 21 (called "Prince of Persia" and "Prince of Greece"); (2) institutional spirits such as those assigned to churches, governments, educational institutions, occult organizations (e.g., Scientology, Freemasonry, Mormonism); non-Christian religions (e.g., the gods of Hinduism, Buddhism, animism); (3) the spirits assigned to oversee and encourage special functions including vices such as prostitution, abortion, homosexuality, gambling, pornography, war, music, cults and the like; (4) spirits assigned to such things as objects, buildings and other spaces as well as nonmaterial entities such as rituals and music; and (5) ancestral spirits, assigned to work with specific families, portraying themselves as ancestors. These spirits working at cosmic level are tightly connected to ground-level family spirits that dwell within the members of a family.

We may diagram these types of spirits as follows:

Cosmic-Level Spirits

1. Territorial Spirits (over territories)

2. Institutional Spirits (over organizations and religions)

3. Special-Function Spirits (over vices)

4. Spirits Attached to Objects, Buildings, Rituals

5. Ancestral Spirits (demons masquerading as ancestors)

Ground-Level Spirits (Living in People)

1. Family Demons (assigned to families, inherited)

2. Occult Demons (representing occult allegiances)

3. Ordinary Demons (attached to sinful attitudes and emotions)

Ground-Level Warfare

An important issue to deal with in every society is ground-level demonization. We should not call this "demon possession," since this term is not a proper translation of the Greek terms which simply mean "have a demon." So, to be true to the Greek and to refrain from giving the impression that the enemy has more power than he, in fact, does, we use the term "demonized" to speak of demons living inside a person.

Jesus frequently encountered and cast out ground-level demons. The Gospels record several accounts of Jesus delivering people from demons. In Mark 1:34 and 3:10–12 it is recorded that Jesus cast demons out of many people. Then, specific attention is given to the freeing of a man with an unclean spirit (Mark 1:23–26), the Gerasene demoniac (Mark 5:1–20) and the dumb man (Matt 9:32–33), plus the report that Mary Magdalene had been demonized (Luke 8:2).

Experience shows that there are a high percentage of people in any society who are hosting demons, especially in societies where babies are dedicated to spirits. In such societies, we can expect the percentage of demonized people to be nearly 100 percent. Only those who for some reason are not dedicated to the spirits (often called gods) might escape.

Experience also shows that demons can live in Christians as well as in non-Christians. I and many of my ministry associates started with the assumption that when a demonized person turns to Christ, the demons have to leave. Unfortunately, our experience with thousands of demonized persons, nearly all of them with undeniable Christian testimonies, has disabused us of this fallacy. What seems to be the case is that, just as sin can live in our soul and body after conversion, so can demons, if they are there when we convert. What seems to be the explanation is that at conversion, our human spirit is made clean both of sin and of demons (if any). Our soul and body, however, need continual attention to root out sin and, if we should be hosting demons, to gain freedom from them (see Kraft, *Defeating Dark Angels*).

Demons can live in people only if they have legal rights granted by what I have called spiritual and emotional "garbage." Such garbage consists of rights given through dedication, through inheritance, through invitation by the person or one in authority over the person, through participation in occult organizations or non-Christian religions with accompanying vows and dedications, through the person wallowing in sin (e.g., adultery, homosexuality, gambling, drunkenness) or holding onto such attitudes as anger, bitterness and unforgiveness, through curses (including self-curses), through murder or attempted murder (including abortion and attempted suicide) and through other, similar ways (see Kraft, *Defeating Dark Angels*). The analogy I use is to say that demons are like rats living in garbage and their strength is calibrated to the amount of garbage in the host. Dealing with the garbage through deep-level prayer ministry, then, is the most important aspect of the process of fighting demons at ground level. Thus, we have found that when we first deal with the garbage in demonized people, we can then deal with the demons easily and effectively without violence (see Kraft, *Deep Wounds*).

Demons work at ground level in ways appropriate to the society in which they are working. They adapt their approach to the problems and concerns most prominent in any given society. Spiritual warfare, therefore, needs to be conducted in recognition of this ability of the enemy to adapt. Though the principle of making negative things worse and getting people to go overboard on positive things seems always to be their way of working, the things they push in each society will differ for maximum effectiveness in Satan's attempts to deceive and disrupt.

In Asian societies, for example, where the relationship between mother-in-law and daughter-in-law is a difficult one, demons will often be active in pushing mothers-in-law to be oppressive and daughters-in-law to hate them. In African societies where fear of the unknown is endemic, demons will push all the buttons they can to increase the fear and scare people into going to diviners (where demonic influence is increased) for relief. In Latin America, Asia and Europe, where male domination of women and children is culturally inculcated, the enemy kingdom is very active in increasing the abuse and the pain felt by women and children. Western secularism, then, with its denial of spiritual reality, allows ground-level demons to run rampant in both Western and Westernizing societies. And we can speak of satanic enhancement of racism and social class oppression in many parts of the world. The thing that all such examples have in common is that the seed from which Satan works to produce harmful fruit is usually culturally appropriate.

One especially fruitful technique used by the enemy in many societies is to infest a family with what we are calling a "family demon" (sometimes referred to as a "familiar spirit" or a "bloodline spirit"). This spirit gets passed down from parents to children generation after generation and is able to invite other spirits into the person. Often a person will harbor a spirit with the name of his/her father's family and also one with the name of his/her mother's family. When, soon after birth, the name and exact date of a Chinese baby's birth is written down and taken to a priest to be registered with the gods of the temple, the rights of the family spirit(s) to the newborn are assured and other spirits associated with the temple may be invited in. These spirits, then, gain strength if, as the child grows up, he/she is taken to a temple or shrine whenever the parents seek healing and/or blessing for the child. Family spirits claim to own the members of "their" family even after a given member has accepted Christ and the demon has been evicted from the person's spirit.

It is often fairly easy to break the power even of long-standing family demons if people first claim Jesus' authority to cancel all rights over the family given by ancestors through vows, curses, dedications, sins, violence or in any other way. They then need to willingly renounce their own dedication to the spirits, including any rights given through any permission they or anyone in authority over them has given enemy spirits during their lifetime (such as receiving healing and/or blessing from these spirits).

What remains, then, is to cancel out the rights given the demons through the creation and retention of spiritual and emotional garbage (e.g., unforgiveness, hatred, anger, shame, rejection, lust, fear, etc.). The major problems in the approach usually stem from the reluctance of persons of many societies (e.g., Asian societies) to admit things that they have done or said that have given rights to the demons. Since God is a God of truth, however, it is necessary for people, no matter what their customs might be, to "come clean" with the things they have done, especially their reactions to things done to them, in order that the heavy loads (Matt 11:28) they produce may be brought to Christ and laid at his feet. When these things are brought to Christ, the demons have nothing more to cling to and usually go quietly at our command.

Though dealing with demons in the authority of Jesus is not difficult, the enemy is active in seeing to it that culturally appropriate excesses are regular occurrences. In America, for example, Satan loves to see to it that stories of big fights with demons (usually by those who don't know what they are doing) get noised abroad (e.g., the movie *The Exorcist*) so that people fear to attempt deliverance. In Korea and Africa, then, it is common to hear of deliverance sessions in which the patient was beaten in an attempt to get the demon out. It is not unknown for people to be killed when such methods are used, thus fulfilling a demon's intent to destroy those he inhabits. Whether by getting people to fear him and, thus, not bother him or by getting them to overdo things, Satan is a master at interfering with and even taking over attempts to defeat him.

The appropriate and proper approach to getting people free from demons in any society seems, however, to always be the same: deal with the spiritual and emotional garbage to weaken the demons, then cast them out. Fighting physically with them is never a good idea and even when restraining the demonized person is required, it is God's power wielded through words rather than through physical force that is most effective.

The Primary Focuses at Ground Level

Contrary to what many assume, the major focus of ground-level warfare has to be on what the enemy attempts to do within us, not outside of us. Our experience with several thousand clients leads us to conclude that Satan's primary concern at ground level is to knock people down in their relationships: with self, with God and with others.

Often the most vicious attacks are on self-image. Prominent in the lives of a majority of our clients is a deep sense of unworthiness, often escalated to self-hate. These people usually have been believing enemy lies concerning who they are, why they are here and the inferiority of their past, present and future attempts to master the game of life. Frequently, these lies spin off from real or perceived feelings that they were unwanted at birth because they were conceived out of wedlock or they were the opposite sex from what their parents wanted. Such feelings, then, whether from such bases or springing from some later life experience (e.g., physical, emotional or sexual abuse) get reinforced throughout life as the person, under pressure from the enemy, focuses on and remembers his or her failures while allowing the memory of successes to fade out of focus. The result is a very low self-image, often in spite of significant accomplishments and a solid relationship with Jesus Christ.

From the enemy's point of view, any time he can get Christians to think less of themselves than God desires, it is time and energy well spent. For, if we ever discover who we are in God's eyes and what we can do to damage Satan's activities when we work together with God in spiritual warfare, engaging in power encounters, we become a serious threat to our enemy. Satan knows what we often forget: human beings are God's masterpiece, much higher in the universe than Satan himself by creation (Gen 1:26; Ps 8:5, correctly translated "a little lower than God," as in the Good News Translation), by redemption (John 5:24; Rom 5:1), by adoption (1 John 3:1; Rom 8:14–17; Gal 4:5–7), through empowerment by the Holy Spirit (Luke 9:1) and in every other way. So his major tactic in relation to us is to keep us from finding out and acting upon these truths.

In addition to our enemy's attempts to disrupt our relationship with self, he gives great attention to the disruption of relationships with others. We have no further to go than to the daily papers and the divorce statistics to calculate the extent of Satan's activity in this area. He knows that the more he disrupts human relationships the more damage he can do to God's masterpiece and to God's plans for us. Behind the baser human propensities listed in several places in Scripture (e.g., Gal 5:19–21; Eph 4:25–31) lie satanic emissaries assigned to tempt, to disrupt friendships, to attack marriages, to sever relationships between parents and children and to bring about miscommunication at all levels.

Demons are also assigned to disrupt our relationship with God. We were made for this relationship and from Satan's first attack on Adam and Eve's intimacy with God to the present, he and his angels have worked full-time to prevent (2 Cor 4:4) or hinder our closeness with our Creator. Satan is undoubtedly behind nominalism and the sapping of meaning from worship, not to mention the various perversions of sound doctrine that keep people from close relationships with God. All of these are important, though perhaps not very glamorous, areas of spiritual warfare.

Cosmic-Level Warfare

Cosmic-level spirits are apparently in charge of ground-level spirits, assigning them to people and supervising them as they carry out their assignments in people or do their tempting and harassing of people from outside of them. Ground-level demons speak of their "assignments," implying that they are under the authority of higher-level satanic beings. I believe it is cosmic-level spirits that Paul refers to as "the wicked spiritual forces in the heavenly world, the rulers, authorities, and cosmic powers of this dark age" (Eph 6:12). Though few biblical scholars doubt the existence of such higher-level spirits, there is a good bit of controversy over what, if anything, we are to do about them since this matter is not fully addressed in Scripture.

The clearest scriptural reference to territorial spirits occurs in Daniel 10 where the angel sent to answer Daniel's prayer speaks of an encounter with the "Prince of Persia" (v. 13) and of an upcoming encounter with the "Prince of Greece" (v. 21). In another reference, the events recorded at the end of 2 Kings 3 (esp. v. 27), are best explained on the assumption that the sacrifice of the son of the king of Moab so empowered satanic territorial spirits that Israel, feeling their power and forgetting to appeal to Yahweh, felt compelled to flee, thus losing a battle they had been clearly winning.

Most of the world believes there are specific spirits attached to nations, regions, mountains, rivers and other geographical features. We find this understanding throughout the Old Testament, where the Baal gods were considered to have control of the plains while Yahweh was supposed to be merely a mountain god. In the events recorded in 1 Kgs 20:23–30, we see Yahweh angered at this belief on the part of the Syrians and, therefore, giving Israel a victory on the plains.

One of the spinoffs of the belief in territorial spirits is the understanding that when people enter the territory of a given god, they need to show respect to that god. We find this practice in the Old Testament where Israel continually gave homage to the Baal gods whom they believed to be in charge of the plains. In 2 Kgs 17:24–28, then, we see the king of Assyria interpreting the difficulties his people who had moved to Israel were having with lions in Israel as attributable to the fact that they didn't know how to show respect to the God of the land of Israel. So he sent priests of Yahweh back to Israel to teach the settlers how to honor Yahweh. This stopped the trouble.

In Hosea 2:8 we see Israel even attributing their prosperity to the Baal gods. Solomon, then, in order to cement relationships with the surrounding countries, both married wives from and erected altars to the gods of Ammon, Moab, Edom and other places to show honor to their countries. In this way he kept peace with these countries by keeping the wives and their relatives happy (1 Kgs 11:1–10). But he damaged his relationship to the true God.

Westerners tend to feel that such beliefs need not be taken seriously since, we believe, these so-called gods are not gods at all but imaginary beings empowered only by superstition. The Bible, however, shows God and his people regarding these gods as satanic spirits and taking them seriously. But we are not to give them worship, thus giving them rights over us, nor to honor or fear them, since the true God is greater and more powerful than these servants of Satan. And, if we are properly related to the true God, we have the authority to protect ourselves from other gods and to confront and defeat them in power encounters when necessary.

Skeptics point out that Jesus seemed not to be concerned with higher-level spirits except in his encounter with Satan himself (Luke 4:1–13). It is likely, however, that when he confronted and defeated Satan in Satan's own territory (i.e., the wilderness was considered the habitation of Satan) Jesus broke much of the devil's power over at least that part of Palestine. Some have suggested, then, that the demons afflicting the Gerasene demoniac (Luke 8:26–33) were territorial spirits. If so, they were concentrated in one man, like ground-level demons, and dealt with in the same way Jesus dealt with spirits whose assignment was purely ground level.

It is my position that our approach to Christian witness needs to recognize the reality of the spirits over the area and gain understanding of their assignments. Often non-Western peoples who recognize that they have been under the sway of territorial spirits for generations have a great deal of understanding of what territory the spirits have influence over and what are the results of this influence. We can, therefore, gain from them valuable insight into how to deal with these spirits as we work with the true God to retake territory that is rightfully his. See Wagner (*Engaging the Enemy*) for case studies dealing with territorial spirits.

Spiritual Mapping

An important spiritual warfare technique developed by George Otis Jr. (*Last of the Giants*), John Dawson (*Taking Our Cities for God*), Ed Silvoso (*That None Should Perish*), C. Peter Wagner (*Warfare Prayer*) and others is called "spiritual mapping." This is an approach to discerning and identifying cosmic-level spirits and the areas, institutions, vices, objects, etc., that they are over as a step toward developing strategies to oppose and defeat them.

Spiritual mapping is much like what God told Ezekiel to do when he commanded him to "get a brick, put it in front of you, and scratch lines on it to represent the city of Jerusalem" (Ezek 4:1). God then told Ezekiel to symbolically (spiritually) attack the city as a message to Israel after which he was to lie on his left side for 390 days and on his right for forty days to symbolically bear the guilt of Israel and Judah. Such mapping is also like what the spies sent into the promised land were told to do to discover what the situation was that Israel would face as they attempted to take the land. Such spying and mapping is a regular practice in physical warfare and provides a major component of the development of the strategies for attacking the enemy. It should certainly be a part of any attempt to engage in cosmic-level spiritual warfare.

Experiments going on in Argentina and elsewhere in the world suggest that a direct approach to warring against cosmic-level spirits can be successful. As with ground-level warfare, the most important part of our strategy needs to be dealing with the spiritual "garbage." At cosmic level, issues of confession of sin, repentance, reconciliation and unity of believers ("corporate garbage") are the first order of business if our praying against territorial bondage is to be successful. The chapter by Ed Silvoso in my book *Behind Enemy Lines* reports on the success of such an approach in Resistencia, Argentina, where he led a three-year comprehensive spiritual attack that started with the breaking of the power of the territorial spirits over the city through authoritative prayer, thus opening the people up for evangelism. That approach involved getting the pastors (the spiritual "gatekeepers") to repent of their sins and their disunity and to unite, training pastors and lay church leaders in praying authoritatively, prayer marching and leading their people in repentance and reconciliation, followed, after two years of such preparation, by all-out evangelism.

The results have been spectacular. Through this effort and those of prominent Argentine evangelists who use this same approach, it appears that much of the satanic blinding spoken of in 2 Cor 4:4 has been broken through. The result has been incredible response to evangelistic efforts issuing in very rapid church growth.

Some have criticized such efforts to wage war at the cosmic-level (e.g., Arnold, *3 Crucial Questions*). They point out that Jesus never seemed to concern himself with any level above ground level. Could it be, though, that the Holy Spirit is simply leading us in our day (the last days?) into some more of the "all truth" that Jesus promised in John 16:13? Or, might it even be that Jesus, by cleaning up so much of the ground-level garbage and praying as much as he did, was contributing greatly to the breaking of satanic power at cosmic level? It seems clear from what those engaged in cosmic-level warfare are discovering that most of what it takes to effectively confront higher-level spirits takes place at ground level. I am referring to such things as confession of sin, repentance, reconciliation and the need for spiritual gatekeepers to work in unity.

Conclusion

Spiritual warfare is a crucial dimension of biblical Christianity. And power encounters are an important part of spiritual warfare. It is a pity that so much of Western Christianity has ignored it for so long. We have seen two levels of spiritual warfare: ground level and cosmic level. With each level the relationship between the spirit realm and the human realm is very close and the way to influence things in the spirit realm is through influencing human behavior. At ground level, dealing with the spiritual and emotional garbage an individual is carrying paves the way for people to get rid of demons. At cosmic level, corporate repentance, reconciliation and Christian unity pave the way for breaking the power of cosmic spirits. In either case, obedience to God is the decisive factor in defeating Satan and those who are living in obedience to him.

Though the Bible is not as specific as we would like it to be at many points, it is clear that God allows no allegiance by his people to enemy spirits, whether they are masquerading as gods or ancestors. Nor does he want us to be deceived by satanic blessings, such as healing or material prosperity or to believe the enemy's lies with regard to reincarnation or the living presence of ancestors. Prohibitions against such things are prominent in the Old Testament and demonstrations and teaching concerning how to use the power of God to overcome both temptation and spirit infestation occur in the New Testament.

In whatever aspect of spiritual warfare we are engaged, we are to seek to experience Jesus and the power of his resurrection (Phil 3:10), learning what the enemy's schemes are (2 Cor 2:11) and waging against him the "good fight" (2 Tim 4:7). Equipping us to defeat the enemy, Jesus, our leader in spiritual warfare, gives us the "power and authority to drive out all demons and to cure diseases" (Luke 9:1; Matt 10:8), promises that "whoever believes in me will do what I do" (John 14:12), sends us into the world as the Father had sent him (John 20:21) and plans to "crush Satan under [our] feet" (Rom 16:20).

BIBLIOGRAPHY

Anderson, Neil. *The Bondage Breaker*. Eugene, OR: Harvest House, 1990.

Arnold, Clinton. *3 Crucial Questions about Spiritual Warfare*. Grand Rapids: Baker, 1997.

Boyd, Gregory. *God at War*. Downers Grove: InterVarsity, 1997.

Brown, Colin, ed. "Curse." In *The New International Dictionary of New Testament Theology*, 1:413–18. Grand Rapids: Zondervan, 1975.

Bubeck, Mark. *The Adversary*. Chicago: Moody, 1975.

———. *Overcoming the Adversary*. Chicago: Moody, 1984.

Burnett, David. *Unearthly Powers*. Eastbourne, UK: Monarch, 1988.

Dawson, John. *Taking Our Cities for God*. Lake Mary, FL: Creation House, 1989.

Dickason, C. Fred. *Demon Possession and the Christian*. Chicago: Moody, 1987.

Hunt, Dave, and T. A. McMahon. *The Seduction of Christianity*. Eugene, OR: Harvest House, 1985.

Kallas, James. *The Satanward View*. Philadelphia: Westminster, 1966.

Kinnaman, Gary D. *Overcoming the Dominion of Darkness*. Grand Rapids: Chosen, 1990.

Kraft, Charles H. *Behind Enemy Lines*. Eugene, OR: Wipf & Stock, 1994.

———. *Christianity with Power*. Grand Rapids: Chosen, 1989.

———. *Deep Wounds, Deep Healing*. Grand Rapids: Chosen, 1993.

———. *Defeating Dark Angels*. Grand Rapids: Chosen, 1992.

———. *I Give You Authority*. Grand Rapids: Chosen, 1997.

———. *The Rules of Engagement*. Eugene, OR: Wipf & Stock, 2000.

Kraft, Marguerite G. *Understanding Spiritual Power*. Maryknoll: Orbis, 1995.

Lehmann, Arthur C., and James E. Myers. *Magic, Witchcraft and Religion*. 4th ed. Mountain View, CA: Mayfield, 1997.

McAll, Kenneth. *Healing the Family Tree*. London: Sheldon, 1982.

Moreau, A. Scott. *Essentials of Spiritual Warfare*. Wheaton: Shaw, 1997.

———. *The World of the Spirits*. Nairobi: Evangel, 1990.

Murphy, Ed. *Handbook for Spiritual Warfare*. Nashville: Nelson, 1992.

Otis, George, Jr. *The Last of the Giants*. Grand Rapids: Chosen, 1991.

Penn-Lewis, Jessie. *War on the Saints*. 9th ed. New York: Lowe, 1973.

Rommen, Edward, ed. *Spiritual Power and Missions*. Pasadena: Carey, 1995.

BIBLIOGRAPHY

Sherman, Dean. *Spiritual Warfare for Every Christian*. Seattle: Frontline, 1990.

Silvoso, Ed. *That None Should Perish*. Grand Rapids: Chosen, 1994.

Tippett, Alan R. *Introduction to Missiology*. Pasadena: Carey, 1987.

———. *People Movements in Southern Polynesia*. Chicago: Moody, 1971.

Wagner, C. Peter. *Confronting the Powers*. Grand Rapids: Chosen, 1996.

———. *Engaging the Enemy*. Grand Rapids: Chosen, 1991.

———. "Territorial Spirits." Chapter 3 in *Wrestling with Dark Angels*, edited by C. Peter Wagner and F. Douglas Pennoyer. Grand Rapids: Chosen, 1990.

———. *Warfare Prayer*. Grand Rapids: Chosen, 1992.

Warner, Timothy. *Spiritual Warfare*. Wheaton: Crossway, 1991.

White, Tom. *The Believer's Guide to Spiritual Warfare*. Grand Rapids: Chosen, 1990.

Wimber, John. *Power Healing*. San Francisco: Harper & Row, 1987.

Wink, Walter. *Engaging the Powers*. Minneapolis: Fortress, 1992.

Lightning Source UK Ltd.
Milton Keynes UK
UKHW022356200922
409144UK00006B/402